ASPA 46 STEP-GUIDE TO BECOMING A SELF-PUBLISHED AUTHOR

BY LEE J DAVIES & ROBERT W JONES

ISBN: 9798871326428

DEDICATION

This book is dedicated to all those taking the first step on this literary journey, may these pages be your compass, guiding you through the labyrinth of self-publishing with wisdom, practical insights, and unwavering support. To the seasoned authors who generously share their knowledge, thank you for lighting the way for those who follow in your footsteps.

Here's to the dreamers who summon worlds from imagination, the storytellers who breathe life into characters, and the resilient souls who embark on the writer's odyssey. May your creativity flow boundlessly, your perseverance endure tirelessly, and your journey as an author unfold with endless wonder.

WELCOME TO ASPA!

Scan the QR code below to Join the community of Self-Publishing Authors today for free.

CONTENTS

INTRODUCTION

Starting a book can be both exciting and overwhelming. You may feel a sense of excitement at the thought of bringing your ideas to life, but also a sense of loneliness and not knowing where to begin.

That's where the Association of Self-Published Authors (ASPA) steps in. Comprising seasoned authors who have traversed the self-publishing terrain, ASPA understands the trials and tribulations that new writers face. We've been in your shoes, grappling with questions about plot, characters, editing, formatting, marketing, and every other facet of the publishing process.

The ASPA 46-Step Guide is the culmination of our collective experience, meticulously distilled into a comprehensive roadmap tailored specifically for authors like you. Our mission is clear: to provide you with a guiding light through the labyrinthine world of self-publishing.

Each of the 46 steps has been carefully crafted to address a specific aspect of the self-publishing journey. From the inception of your idea to the moment you hold your finished book in your hands, ASPA is here to offer expert guidance, practical advice, and unwavering support.

Throughout this guide, you will find invaluable insights, actionable tips, and resources that will empower you to make informed decisions and confidently navigate the challenges that lie ahead. Whether you're struggling with plot development, formatting dilemmas, or marketing strategies, ASPA has your back.

As you embark on this transformative journey, remember that you are not alone. The ASPA community, alongside this guide, serves as a steadfast companion, cheering you on from the side lines and celebrating every milestone you reach. We believe in your story, and we are committed to helping you share it with the world.

So, dear writer, take a deep breath and step boldly onto the path of self-publishing. With ASPA by your side, you have the tools, knowledge, and support to turn your literary dreams into reality. Embrace the adventure, and let's embark on this incredible journey together. Your story deserves to be told, and we are honoured to be a part of your narrative.

This is where it all starts – I think I would like to write a book...

Congratulations on starting your journey! It may not seem like you have achieved that much but by reading this you will have already decided that you would like to become an author and are interested in knowing how to be one.

Conception of an Idea

The journey of writing a book often begins with a spark of inspiration. It can be a fleeting thought, a vivid dream, or an experience that lingers in the mind. At first, the idea is like a flickering flame, casting a warm glow on the imagination. Excitement and enthusiasm mix with a sense of uncertainty, as you grapple with the enormity of the task ahead.

The Swirling Thoughts and Feelings

As the idea takes root, a whirlwind of thoughts and emotions accompanies it. Doubts may arise, questioning if the concept is strong enough, or if you possess the necessary skills to see it through. Simultaneously, there's a palpable sense of anticipation, a yearning to bring this idea to life and share it with the world.

The Daunting Blank Canvas

When faced with a blank page or screen, the enormity of the task can be overwhelming. The path forward may seem uncertain, and the process of turning a nebulous concept into a tangible story can be intimidating. Questions linger in your mind: Where do I start? How do I structure this? Which words will best convey my vision?

Navigating Trust and Disclosure

The fear of sharing your idea with others is common. You wonder: Who can I trust with this precious creation? Will they understand its potential, or will it be met with indifference? The vulnerability of entrusting your vision to someone else can be daunting, yet it's an essential step in the journey towards publication.

Paving the Path to Publication

The road to becoming a published author is riddled with uncertainties. Traditional publishing routes may seem elusive, and self-publishing may feel like uncharted territory. The prospect of marketing and distribution looms, and the intricacies of copyright and legalities add an additional layer of complexity.

Don’t worry though as this guide will support you one step at a time.

STEP 1 – CHOOSING YOUR PATH

Writing Your Own Book. Seeking Support. Or, Ghost-writing.

Embarking on the journey of writing a book is a significant endeavor, and it's essential to determine the approach that aligns best with your vision and capabilities. There are three primary paths you can take: writing the book yourself, seeking support from an author or editor, or enlisting the expertise of a ghost-writer. Each option presents its own set of advantages and considerations.

1. Writing Your Own Book

Pros:

- **Personal Expression:** Writing your own book allows you to fully express your unique voice, ideas, and experiences.
- **Complete Creative Control:** You have full control over the plot, characters, themes, and style of your book.
- **Satisfaction of Accomplishment:** Completing a book on your own can be an incredibly rewarding and fulfilling experience.

Cons:

- **Learning Curve:** Writing requires honing a set of skills that may take time and practice to develop.
- **Time-Intensive:** It can be a time-consuming process, particularly if you have a busy schedule.
- **Potential for Writer's Block:** There may be moments of creative stagnation that can be challenging to overcome.

2. Seeking Support from an Author or Editor

Pros:

- **Guidance and Expertise:** Collaborating with an experienced author or editor provides access to valuable insights, feedback, and professional advice.
- **Improved Quality:** A seasoned professional can help refine your ideas, enhance your writing, and ensure a polished final product.
- **Structured Process:** Working with a support figure can provide a structured framework, making the writing process more manageable.

Cons:

- **Potential for Creative Differences:** There may be moments of creative divergence, which require effective communication and compromise. Be careful with who you work with to edit your work so that you do not lose your voice or your story.
- **Financial Investment:** Engaging a professional for support may involve a financial commitment.

3. Ghost-writing

Pros:

- **Efficiency:** Ghost-writers are skilled in bringing ideas to life quickly and efficiently, which can save you substantial time.

- **Expertise in Writing Craft:** Ghost-writers are often seasoned professionals with a deep understanding of storytelling and writing techniques.
- **Maintained Anonymity:** If desired, you can keep the fact that a ghost-writer was involved confidential.

Cons:

- **Limited Personal Involvement:** You relinquish some creative control and personal connection to the writing process.
- **Financial Investment:** Engaging a ghost-writer typically involves a significant financial commitment.

Ultimately, the path you choose depends on your individual goals, preferences, and resources. There is no one-size-fits-all approach to writing a book, and it's perfectly valid to explore each option before deciding. Whichever path you select, remember that the journey of writing a book is a highly personal and gratifying experience, and the result is a testament to your creativity and determination.

RESOURCES

Some resources that can provide help and support with the options listed above are as follows:

Meet The Authors(http://meettheauthors.net)

Provides support for all of these paths, their Solo author (DIY) 6-week Boot Camp package provides all of the support and information you need to learn how to become a best-selling author. With weekly video discussions you will be able to learn from other others who have experienced the many pitfalls that many authors fall fowl of.

The Collaboration package provides you with support on your book with, reviews and edits as well as guidance and mentoring so that you feel supported throughout the process.

Their Ghost Writer package is an affordable option in comparison to many other Ghost-writers which entails you providing your story over a series of video calls. This will then be transferred to your own book or memoir and includes book cover design, publishing, and printing.

Reedsy (https://reedsy.com) Reedsy offers a marketplace for authors to find and hire professional editors, proof-readers, and other publishing professionals.

Scribendi (https://www.scribendi.com) Scribendi is a professional editing and proofreading service with a team of experienced editors.

Upwork (https://www.upwork.com) Upwork is a freelancing platform where you can find a wide range of freelance editors and proof-readers.

Freelancer (https://www.freelancer.com) Similar to Upwork, Freelancer is a platform where you can post your project and receive bids from freelance editors and proof-readers.

fiverr.

Fiverr (https://www.fiverr.com) Fiverr is a platform where you can find freelancers offering a variety of services, including editing and proofreading.

STEP 2 – DECIDING ON A GENRE

Having a clear understanding of the genre in which you're writing is paramount to creating a compelling and engaging book. The genre sets the stage for your narrative, shaping the reader's expectations and providing a framework for your storytelling. Here are some key considerations to keep in mind:

1. Familiarise Yourself with Genre Conventions:

- Each genre comes with its own set of conventions, whether it's the fast-paced action of a thriller or the intricate world-building of science fiction. Understanding these conventions allows you to effectively employ and, if needed, subvert them to create a unique and engaging story.

2. Identify Your Target Audience:

- Different genres appeal to different demographics and reader preferences. Knowing your target audience helps you tailor your writing style, themes, and narrative elements to resonate with your intended readership.

3. Study Exemplary Works:

- Immerse yourself in notable works within your chosen genre. This not only provides inspiration but also offers valuable insights into successful narrative structures, character development, and thematic elements specific to that genre.

4. Pay Attention to Themes and Tropes:

- Genres often have recurring themes and tropes that readers expect to encounter. Understanding these allows you to use them effectively, or, if you choose, to challenge and subvert them to create a fresh and unique narrative.

5. Maintain Consistency:

- Within a genre, there's an implicit contract with the reader about the kind of experience they can expect. It's crucial to maintain consistency in tone, style, and pacing to meet these expectations and provide a satisfying reading experience.

6. Blend Genres Thoughtfully (If Applicable):

- While genres provide a framework, don't be afraid to blend elements from different genres if it serves your story. However, it's essential to do so thoughtfully, ensuring that the fusion enhances the narrative rather than confuses or dilutes it.

7. Be Mindful of Genre Trends:

- Literary trends evolve over time. Staying aware of current trends can help you position your work in a way that appeals to contemporary readers while still offering a unique and fresh perspective.

8. Understand Subgenres and Crossovers:

- Many genres have subcategories or can overlap with others. Understanding these distinctions can help you refine your writing to fit more precisely within a specific niche or blend elements from multiple genres seamlessly.

In summary, a clear understanding of your chosen genre provides a solid foundation for crafting a compelling narrative. It not only helps you meet reader expectations but also empowers you to innovate within the established framework. Embrace the unique opportunities and challenges that your chosen genre presents, and let it guide you toward creating a memorable and impactful book.

An example of the most common genres can be seen below:

1. Fiction
2. Mystery
3. Thriller
4. Science Fiction
5. Fantasy
6. Horror
7. Romance
8. Historical Fiction
9. Adventure
10. Dystopian
11. Young Adult (YA)
12. Children's
13. Middle Grade
14. Paranormal
15. Crime
16. Suspense
17. Non-Fiction
18. Biography/Autobiography
19. Memoir
20. Self-Help
21. Psychology
22. Philosophy
23. Spirituality
24. Religion
25. Science
26. Nature
27. Travel
28. Food and Cooking
29. Health and Wellness
30. Fitness
31. Parenting
32. Education
33. Reference
34. How-to Guides
35. DIY/Crafts

36. Art and Photography
37. Poetry
38. Drama/Play
39. Humour
40. Satire
41. Anthology
42. Short Stories
43. Essays
44. Mystery/Crime Anthology
45. Science Fiction/Fantasy Anthology
46. Romance Anthology
47. Historical Fiction Anthology
48. Poetry Collection
49. Graphic Novel/Comic
50. Graphic Memoir

STEP 3 – COLLECTING YOUR IDEAS

Before embarking on the journey of writing a book, it's essential to gather and organise your ideas. This crucial step lays the foundation for a coherent and engaging narrative. Here are effective strategies for collecting and harnessing your creative thoughts:

1. **Keep a Journal or Notebook:**
    - Carry a small notebook or use a note-taking app to capture fleeting thoughts, interesting observations, or snippets of dialogue. These fragments often become the building blocks of your story.
2. **Utilise Digital Tools:**
    - Leverage digital tools like Evernote, OneNote, or even a simple text document to store and organise your ideas. Create folders or categories to sort ideas by theme, character, setting, or plot.
3. **Mind Mapping or Brainstorming:**
    - Use mind maps or brainstorming sessions to visually explore connections between different elements of your story. This technique can help you see the bigger picture and uncover hidden possibilities.
4. **Set Up an Idea Board:**
    - Create a physical or digital board where you can pin or post images, articles, or notes that inspire you. Visual cues can be powerful prompts for creativity.

5. Record Dreams and Daydreams:

- Pay attention to your dreams and daydreams. They often contain unique and unexpected elements that can add depth and originality to your narrative.

6. Read Widely and Take Notes:

- Reading a diverse range of books exposes you to different styles, perspectives, and storytelling techniques. Take notes on what resonates with you and consider how these elements might influence your own work.

7. Explore Personal Experiences:

- Draw on your own life experiences, emotions, and challenges. Personal anecdotes can serve as a rich source of material, providing authenticity and depth to your writing.

8. Conduct Research:

- For genres that require a degree of factual accuracy, research is crucial. Collect articles, books, and interviews related to your subject matter to ensure your writing is informed and credible.

9. Use Writing Prompts:

- Writing prompts can be a fun and effective way to stimulate creativity. They provide a starting point for generating new ideas or exploring different aspects of your story.

10. Engage in Creative Exercises:

- Participate in exercises like free writing, character interviews, or setting descriptions. These activities can help you uncover hidden facets of your story and characters.

11. Seek Inspiration in Nature and the Environment:

- Spend time outdoors, observe natural landscapes, and absorb the sensory experiences. Nature often provides a wellspring of inspiration for settings, moods, and themes.

12. Embrace Randomness:

- Sometimes, allowing your mind to wander aimlessly or engaging in random activities can lead to unexpected and brilliant ideas. Trust the creative process and be open to spontaneity.

Remember, the process of collecting ideas is highly personal. Experiment with different techniques to find what works best for you. As your collection of ideas grows, review and refine them regularly. This ensures you're equipped with an abundance of inspiration when it's time to begin writing your book.

STEP 4 – CREATING A HIGH-LEVEL PLAN

Having a high-level summary before embarking on the writing process is akin to having a roadmap before a long journey. It serves as a guiding beacon, providing direction and purpose to your creative endeavours. Firstly, a well-crafted summary helps to crystallise your ideas and refine your vision. It forces you to distil the essence of your story, honing in on the key plot points, characters, and themes. This clarity not only prevents aimless wandering during the writing process but also ensures that each element in your narrative serves a purpose, contributing to the overarching story arc.

Furthermore, a high-level summary acts as a strategic tool in the writing process. It enables you to maintain a clear sense of focus and prevents you from straying too far from your original intentions. It becomes a touchstone you can refer back to, especially when the creative process gets challenging or convoluted. This not only saves time but also maintains the integrity of your narrative. It's like a lighthouse, helping you navigate through the vast sea of ideas and potential plotlines.

Beyond the creative process, a high-level summary serves a multitude of practical purposes. It becomes an invaluable tool for pitching your book to agents, publishers, or potential readers. This succinct overview communicates the essence of your story, offering a tantalising glimpse into what readers can expect. It's a powerful marketing tool, that helps you generate interest and secure support for your project. It provides a sturdy foundation upon which you can build a compelling and cohesive narrative, ultimately enhancing the quality and impact of your book.

The free ASPA high-level book summary tool can be used to capture your plan and be downloaded below.

STEP 5 – PROTECTING YOUR IDEA

Having a Non-Disclosure Agreement (NDA) is paramount when you have a new book idea, as it safeguards your intellectual property and preserves your creative control. An NDA establishes a legally binding contract between you and anyone you share your idea with, ensuring that they cannot disclose, reproduce, or profit from your concept without your consent. This is crucial in the competitive world of publishing, where unique and innovative ideas are highly valued.

Furthermore, an NDA instils confidence in potential collaborators, publishers, and investors. Knowing that their involvement won't lead to unauthorized sharing or duplication of your concept, they are more likely to engage with you in discussions and partnerships. It creates a professional and respectful environment, allowing you to share your vision with peace of mind, knowing that your idea is protected. In the fast-paced and dynamic world of literature, where ideas can be easily replicated, an NDA serves as a fortress around your creative work, enabling you to navigate the industry with confidence and security.

For a new author looking to protect their idea, an NDA should include the following key elements:

1. **Introduction of Parties**: Clearly state the names and contact information of both parties involved. The Disclosing Party is the one sharing the confidential

information, and the Receiving Party is the one receiving it.

2. **Definition of Confidential Information**: Provide a specific and detailed definition of what constitutes confidential information. In the context of a new author, this would encompass the book idea, plot, characters, settings, and any other proprietary elements related to the work.
3. **Purpose of Disclosure**: Clearly state the purpose for which the confidential information is being shared. In this case, it would be for the purpose of seeking feedback, collaboration, or any other specified purpose related to the development or publication of the book.
4. **Obligations of Receiving Party**: Outline the responsibilities of the Receiving Party regarding the confidential information. This may include a commitment not to disclose, reproduce, or use the information for any purpose other than the stated purpose.
5. **Exclusions from Confidentiality**: Specify any information that is not covered by the confidentiality agreement. This could include information that is already publicly available or becomes public knowledge through no fault of the Receiving Party.
6. **Duration of Confidentiality**: Define the period during which the confidentiality obligations will be in effect. This could be for a specific duration (e.g., two years) or until a specific event occurs (e.g., publication of the book).
7. **Return or Destruction of Information**: Specify what should happen to the confidential information once the purpose of the disclosure has been fulfilled. This may include returning any physical documents or deleting digital files containing the confidential

information.

8. **Exceptions to Confidentiality**: Detail any circumstances under which the Receiving Party may be required or permitted to disclose the confidential information. This could include legal obligations, court orders, or government requests.
9. **No License or Ownership**: Clarify that the disclosure of confidential information does not grant any rights, licenses, or ownership of the information to the Receiving Party.
10. **Remedies for Breach**: Specify the consequences that may result from a breach of the NDA, including potential legal action and remedies available to the Disclosing Party.
11. **Governing Law and Jurisdiction**: Indicate which jurisdiction's laws will govern the agreement and where any legal disputes will be resolved.
12. **Entire Agreement**: State that the NDA constitutes the entire agreement between the parties and supersedes any prior agreements or understandings.

It is advisable to consult with a legal professional to ensure that the NDA is tailored to your specific needs and complies with local laws and regulations. Additionally, both parties should carefully read and understand the terms of the NDA before signing it.

STEP 6 – GET FEEDBACK ON YOUR IDEA

When it comes to sharing your idea for a new book with friends and family, it's important to select individuals you trust implicitly. Look for those who not only respect your creative boundaries but also have a proven track record of discretion. This foundation of trust forms the basis for a secure and constructive feedback loop.

When discussing your concept, seek out individuals who won't merely echo your sentiments but will provide honest and constructive critiques. These are the people who challenge your thinking, ask probing questions, and offer perspectives you might not have considered. Their feedback is invaluable, as it can expose potential weaknesses in your idea or illuminate avenues for improvement.

Listening to and incorporating this feedback is a vital part of the creative process. It allows you to refine and strengthen your concept, shaping it into a more compelling and robust narrative. However, it's crucial to maintain a discerning ear, filtering through feedback and integrating what aligns with your vision while discarding suggestions that may dilute your originality.

Ultimately, the balance lies in finding individuals who respect your creative rights while providing candid, constructive feedback. This blend of trust and critical insight can be a powerful force in honing your idea into a truly exceptional book.

STEP 7 – PLAN YOUR CHARACTERS

Planning characters for a book or novel is a crucial step in creating a compelling and engaging story. Here are some key steps and considerations:

1. **Character Profiles:**
Start by creating detailed character profiles for each major character. Include their name, age, physical appearance, background, personality traits, likes, dislikes, and any significant life events that have shaped them.

2. **Motivations and Goals:**
Understand what drives your characters. What are their short-term and long-term goals? What are their deepest desires or fears? Knowing their motivations will inform their actions and decisions throughout the story.

3. **Complexity and Flaws:**
Characters should be multi-dimensional. Give them strengths, weaknesses, quirks, and flaws. This adds depth and relatability to their personalities.

4. **Backstories:**
Craft detailed backstories for your characters, even if only a fraction of it makes it into the final narrative. Understanding their history helps you write more convincingly and consistently.

5. **Roles and Relationships:**
Consider how each character fits into the larger narrative. What is their role in the story? How do they relate to other characters? Are they allies, adversaries, or something in between?

6. **Conflict and Development:**
Identify the conflicts and challenges each character will face. This can be external (e.g., a villain, a natural disaster) or internal (e.g., personal doubts, moral dilemmas). Characters should evolve and grow over the course of the story.

7. **Dialogue and Voice:**
Each character should have a distinct way of speaking. Consider their education level, regional dialect, and any unique speech patterns. This helps differentiate their voices in dialogue.

8. **Visual Aids (Optional):**
Create visual aids like mood boards or sketches to help visualize your characters. This can be especially useful for their physical appearance and style.

9. **Consistency:**
Keep a record of your characters' details to ensure consistency throughout the narrative. This includes aspects like eye colour, habits, and speech patterns.

10. **Emotional Range:**
Characters should display a range of emotions. Consider how they express joy, anger, sadness, and other feelings. This makes them more relatable and human.

11. **Symbolism (Optional):**
Think about whether your characters represent larger themes or ideas within your story. This can add depth and layers to their significance.
Remember, while planning is crucial, characters can also evolve as you write. Stay open to new insights and developments that may arise during the creative process. This can lead to even more authentic and dynamic characters in your final work.

RESOURCES

Some resources that may be able to help are listed below:

Meet The Authors Book Planning tool.

The **become an author 6 week bootcamp package** and the **author collaboration package** both provide various resources to help authors along every step of the process. One of the downloads is a really useful Book planner that includes a chapter tracker, a character list, chapter summary, locations list and research section.

Price: Full 6 Week author bootcamp only £185.
Get your book edited and access all available tools in the collaboration package only £1499.

Plottr is a specialised book planning tool tailored primarily for fiction writers. This software empowers you to c
raft a comprehensive blueprint of your narrative, spanning chapters, plots, characters, and more. Developed with the ethos of "by writers for writers," this visual outlining tool streamlines the often-cumbersome process of structuring your book.
It's worth noting that Plottr does not include a dedicated space for drafting. However, after fashioning your outline in Plottr, you can seamlessly export it to serve as the guiding framework for your draft writing phase.
PriceLifetime licence between $39 for 1 device.
to $299 pro version.

STEP 8 – MAKE A BOOK PLANNER

Having a comprehensive book plan is the cornerstone of a successful and well-crafted narrative. It serves as the roadmap that guides the author through the intricacies of storytelling. Here are some crucial elements that a thorough book plan encompasses:

Character Development:
A well-detailed plan outlines the main characters, their backgrounds, motivations, and arcs. This ensures that characters are multi-dimensional and evolve throughout the story.

Chapter Outlines:
Structuring the book into chapters provides a clear framework for pacing and progression. Each chapter should have a purpose, advancing the plot or revealing important information.

Scene Descriptions:
Describing scenes helps set the stage, providing the reader with a vivid visual of the setting. It also allows for seamless transitions between locations.

Interactions and Conversations:
Planning interactions and dialogues ensure they serve a purpose in advancing the plot or developing characters. This prevents aimless or redundant exchanges.

Location Details:
Detailed descriptions of locations immerse the reader in the

story's world. Understanding the physical environment helps create a vivid and immersive reading experience.

Relationship Dynamics:
Defining relationships between characters is crucial. This includes family ties, friendships, conflicts, and romantic entanglements. These dynamics drive character motivations and actions.

Plot Points and Twists:
The book plan should include key plot points, including the inciting incident, rising action, climax, and resolution. It should also account for any unexpected twists or turns.

Research and References:
Depending on the genre, research may be necessary to ensure accuracy and authenticity. This could involve historical facts, scientific details, or cultural nuances

Theme Integration:
The plan should incorporate the overarching themes or messages of the book. This ensures that every element of the story serves to reinforce or explore these themes.

Foreshadowing and Symbolism:
Planning for foreshadowing and symbolic elements adds depth to the narrative. It provides a layer of meaning that discerning readers can uncover.

Tension and Conflict:
The plan should strategically place moments of tension and conflict to keep the story engaging and the reader invested in the outcome.

Character Arcs and Development:
It's important to outline how each character evolves throughout the story. This includes their growth, the challenges they face, and how they are transformed by the events.

By meticulously detailing these elements in a book plan, authors create a solid foundation for their writing process. It helps maintain focus and coherence and ensures that every component of the story serves a purpose in the overall narrative. This level of preparedness ultimately leads to a more compelling and satisfying reading experience for the audience.

RESOURCES

There are not many book planning tools available currently. The websites below have online tools to help plan your book as part of their overall software but do not provide just the planner separately. Also please be aware of the cost to sign up to these.

Scrivener: If you're using Scrivener for writing, it also includes built-in templates for organizing your book project.
Scrivener | Literature & Latte (literatureandlatte.com)

Trello or Asana: While not specifically for book planning, project management tools like Trello or Asana can be adapted for this purpose. You can create boards or tasks for different aspects of your book project
Manage Your Team's Projects From Anywhere | Trello

Meet The Authors Book Planning tool.

MTA provide an easy-to-use specifically designed book planning tool which enables you to structure your book and provide you guidance with character and scene mapping.

This can be purchased for £4.99 here

STEP 9 – START YOUR RESEARCH

Effective research is a cornerstone of creating a well-informed and believable narrative in a book. Here are some techniques for conducting research when writing:

Define Your Research Goals:
Begin by clearly defining what you need to know. This could involve historical facts, cultural details, technical knowledge, or any other specific information relevant to your book.

Diverse Sources:
Utilise a wide range of sources, including books, articles, academic papers, interviews, documentaries, and credible websites. This ensures a comprehensive understanding of your subject matter.

Libraries and Archives:
Physical libraries and archives offer a wealth of information. Librarians can be invaluable resources in guiding your research and helping you locate relevant materials.

Online Databases and Journals:
Access online databases and academic journals for in-depth and specialised information. These resources often provide peer-reviewed and credible sources.

Interview Experts or Witnesses:
Talking to experts, professionals, or individuals with first-hand experience can provide unique insights and authentic details that might not be found in written sources.

Field Research:
If possible, visit locations relevant to your book. This provides first-hand experiences and sensory details that can enhance the authenticity of your narrative.

Document Everything:
Keep meticulous records of your research, including citations, quotes, and reference materials. This ensures accuracy and allows you to easily refer back to sources.

Fact-Checking:
Verify the information you gather from multiple sources to ensure accuracy and reliability. This is especially important for historical or technical details.

Use Specialised Search Engines:
Utilise specialised search engines or databases relevant to your topic. For example, academic search engines like Google Scholar can provide scholarly articles and papers.

Join Forums or Groups:
Online forums and communities related to your subject matter can be excellent places to ask questions, exchange ideas, and gather insights from a community of experts or enthusiasts.

Government Publications and Reports:
Government websites often provide a wealth of statistical and information. Reports, studies, and official documents can be valuable resources.

Maintain a Research Calendar:
Set aside specific times for research and allocate enough time to delve deeply into your subject matter. Consistency in research efforts is key.

Avoid Information Overload:
While it's important to be thorough, be mindful of not drowning

in an excess of information. Focus on gathering what is directly relevant to your narrative.

Remember to approach your research with a critical eye and evaluate the credibility of your sources. The goal is to build a foundation of accurate information that supports the authenticity and depth of your narrative.

STEP 10 – START TO WRITE

This is it! The moment you've been building up to, and for some the first step that they have taken. Starting the first chapter of a book can be both exhilarating and daunting. Here are some techniques to help you get started and navigate the emotions that may accompany this crucial beginning:

Begin with a Compelling Hook:
Engage your reader from the very first sentence. A captivating hook can be a thought-provoking question, a vivid description, or a surprising statement that piques curiosity.

Establish the Setting and Tone:
Quickly immerse your reader in the world of your story. Describe the setting, atmosphere, and mood to create a vivid and immediate sense of place.

Introduce a Central Character or Situation:
Introduce a character or a situation that will be central to the narrative. This creates an anchor for the reader to latch onto and invest in.

Convey a Sense of Purpose or Conflict:
Establish what is at stake for your characters. Whether it's a personal goal, a challenge they face, or a larger conflict, make it clear why the reader should care about what happens.

Show, Don't Just Tell:
Engage the reader's senses and emotions by showing actions, thoughts, and feelings rather than simply telling them. This creates a more immersive experience.

Balance Description and Action:
Find the right balance between descriptive passages and action. Too much description can slow down the pacing, while too much action without context can be disorienting.

Write Freely, Edit Later:
Allow yourself to write freely without getting bogged down by perfectionism. You can refine and edit later. The first draft is about getting your ideas down on paper.

Listen to Your Instincts:
Trust your intuition and creative instincts. If a certain direction feels right, follow it. You can always revise or adjust later if needed.

Embrace Uncertainty and Excitement:
It's normal to feel a mix of excitement and uncertainty when starting a new chapter. Embrace this energy and let it fuel your creativity.

Set Realistic Goals:
Establish achievable writing goals for each session. This could be a word count, a specific scene, or a particular event you want to cover.

Connect with Your Characters:
Understand your characters' perspectives and motivations. This will inform their actions and reactions, making them more relatable and engaging.

Consider Multiple Beginnings:
Don't be afraid to try out different opening scenes or approaches. Sometimes, experimenting with different beginnings can lead to discovering the most effective one.

Remember, the first chapter sets the tone for your entire book. It's a powerful opportunity to draw readers in and make them eager to continue. Trust in your storytelling abilities and enjoy the process of bringing your narrative to life.

STEP 11 – FIND SOMEONE TO BOUNCE IDEAS OFF

Finding a trusted confidant to discuss and refine your ideas for a new book is an invaluable step in the creative process. Here are some considerations and suggestions for identifying the right person:

Seek Someone with Expertise:
Look for individuals with relevant experience or knowledge in writing, literature, or a related field. This could be a teacher, fellow author, editor, or someone with a background in your book's subject matter.

Value Their Opinion:
Choose someone whose opinion you respect and trust. This person should be capable of providing constructive feedback and insights that will enhance your work.

Consider Their Availability:
Ensure that the person you choose has the time and willingness to engage in meaningful discussions about your book. Availability for regular meetings or correspondence is important.

Emphasize Honesty and Constructive Criticism:
Look for someone who will be candid in their feedback. While support is important, it's equally crucial to have someone who will point out areas for improvement.

Align with Your Creative Vision:
Seek out individuals who share a similar vision or appreciation for the genre or themes you're exploring. This can lead to more meaningful and relevant feedback.

Confidentiality and Trustworthiness:
Choose someone you can trust to keep your ideas and discussions confidential. This ensures that your creative work remains protected.

Open-Mindedness and Respect:
Find someone who is open to different ideas and perspectives. They should respect your creative autonomy while offering valuable insights.

Mutual Respect for Each Other's Work:
Ideally, this person should also be open to sharing their own work or ideas. A mutually beneficial creative exchange can be incredibly enriching.

Professionalism and Experience:
If possible, seek out individuals who have professional experience in the writing or publishing industry. Their insights can be particularly valuable.

Test the Waters:
Start with a casual discussion or share a small excerpt to gauge their response and compatibility as a sounding board. Pay attention to the quality of feedback and the level of engagement.

Clear Communication:
Choose someone with whom you can communicate effectively. Clear and constructive communication is crucial for productive brainstorming and feedback sessions.
Remember, the person you choose should be someone whose input you value and who genuinely supports your creative endeavours. They should be a trusted partner in your creative process, helping you refine and bring your ideas to fruition.

Online there are various courses designed to help you look into what types of books are selling on Amazon the most and the most popular genres etc however it appears that only Meet The Authors offers a pitching service where you can provide details of your ides (Under full non-disclosure protection) and gain actionable feedback.

RESOURCES

Meet The Authors Pitch it service

Secure story-pitching service. Before the informative 30-minute Teams or Zoom call, they will furnish you with a signed Non-Disclosure Agreement (NDA) to safeguard your concept. Rest assured; your idea will be treated with utmost confidentiality.
Post-call, they will offer valuable feedback on your concept, assessing its distinctiveness, identifying the target audience, and evaluating its credibility. Additionally, they may provide suggestions on how to enhance and diversify the narrative.

Price £50

Click here for more information

STEP 12 – START TO LOOK AT PROOF-READERS AND EDITING

As a new author, one of the most crucial decisions you'll face is whether to enlist the services of a proof-reader or an editor. Both play vital roles in refining your manuscript, but they serve different functions in the writing process.

1.Understanding the Difference: Proof-reader vs. Editor

Proof-reader:
Focuses on correcting grammar, spelling, punctuation, and minor typographical errors.
Ensures consistency in language and formatting.
Verifies that your work adheres to style guides or specific publishing requirements.

Editor:
Engages in a comprehensive review of your manuscript, focusing on overall structure, clarity, coherence, and style.
Offers feedback on character development, plot progression, dialogue, and pacing.
Provides suggestions for improving language flow, narrative voice, and thematic coherence.

2. Reflecting on Your Needs

Consider the stage of your manuscript and your own writing strengths:

Proofreading might be the priority if you've already revised extensively and feel confident in your storytelling abilities but want a final polish for minor errors.

Editing is crucial if you're seeking comprehensive feedback on the overall quality and coherence of your work, especially if it's a first draft.

3. Researching Proof-readers and Editors

When seeking professional help, it's essential to conduct thorough research to find the right fit for your project:

Online Directories and Freelance Platforms:
Websites like Reedsy, Upwork, and Freelancer allow you to browse profiles and reviews of experienced proof-readers and editors.

Recommendations and Referrals:
Seek advice from fellow writers, writing groups, or writing associations. Personal recommendations can be invaluable.

Portfolio Review:
Examine samples of their previous work to ensure their style aligns with your vision for your manuscript.

Communication and Compatibility:
Reach out to potential proof-readers or editors to discuss your project, timelines, and pricing. Gauge their responsiveness and professionalism.

4. Budget Considerations

Balancing Quality and Budget:
Determine a budget that aligns with your goals and the level of expertise you require. Remember that investing in quality editing can significantly enhance the marketability of your book.

5. Sample Edit or Proof

Request a Sample:
Many professional proof-readers and editors offer a sample edit or proofread. This allows you to assess their style, approach, and compatibility with your writing.

In conclusion, choosing whether to use a proof-reader or an editor is a pivotal step in the publishing process. Careful consideration of your manuscript's needs, research into potential professionals, and effective communication will contribute to a successful partnership. Remember, the ultimate goal is to bring out the best in your work and present it to the world in the most polished form possible.

STEP 13 – CHAPTER CRITIQUING

Critiquing your own book chapters is a valuable part of the self- editing process. It helps you identify areas that need improvement, consistency issues, and opportunities for strengthening your writing. Here's a step-by-step guide on how to do a chapter critique on your own book:

Take a Break: Like self-proofreading, it's essential to take a break between writing the chapter and critiquing it. This break allows you to approach the work with fresh eyes.

Read the Chapter: Start by reading the entire chapter without making any edits. Pay attention to the flow, pacing, and your initial emotional response as a reader.

Identify the Chapter's Purpose: Consider the purpose of the chapter within the context of your novel. Is it advancing the plot, developing characters, or providing important background information? Ensure that every chapter serves a clear purpose.

Character Consistency: Check that your characters' actions, motivations, and dialogue are consistent with their established traits and arcs throughout the story. Make sure they react to events in a believable way.

Plot Progression: Analyse whether the chapter advances the plot or contributes to the overall story arc. Eliminate any sections that don't move the narrative.

Dialogue Evaluation: Assess the quality of the dialogue in the chapter. It should sound natural and reveal character traits, move the plot, or provide necessary information. Eliminate any unnecessary or redundant dialogue.

Setting and Description: Ensure that your descriptions are vivid and help readers visualize the settings and characters. Avoid overloading the text with excessive detail but provide enough to create an immersive experience.

Show vs. Tell: Examine whether you're showing the reader important information through actions, dialogue, and sensory details, or if you're telling them outright. Showing is often more engaging and immersive.

Consistency and Logic: Check for consistency in details, such as time of day, weather, and the physical environment. Ensure that the events in the chapter make logical sense within the story's world.

Emotional Impact: Assess whether the chapter elicits the intended emotional responses from the reader. Is it engaging, suspenseful, emotional, or thought-provoking as needed for the context?

Check for Repetition: Be vigilant for redundant information, repeated phrases, or ideas that you've already conveyed in earlier chapters. Eliminate anything that doesn't add value.

Get Feedback: If possible, share the chapter with critique partners or beta readers for their input. They can offer valuable insights and perspectives that you might have missed.

Make Revisions: Based on your analysis and any feedback received, make the necessary revisions. Rewrite sentences, reorganise paragraphs, and eliminate anything that doesn't contribute to the chapter's effectiveness.

Repeat the Process: Once you've critiqued and revised the chapter, repeat this process for each subsequent chapter in your book.

Remember that self-critiquing is an iterative process, and it's okay to go through multiple rounds of revisions. It's also beneficial to set the chapter aside and revisit it later to ensure that you've made the right improvements. Ultimately, your goal is to create a cohesive and engaging narrative throughout your book.

STEP 14 – FINISH YOUR DRAFT VERSION OF YOUR BOOK

For many writers, finishing the first draft of a book can be an exhilarating and emotional experience. After months or even years of hard work, seeing your story take shape on the page can bring a sense of pride and accomplishment. At the same time, finishing a first draft can also be daunting. It's easy to feel overwhelmed by the task of editing and revising, and many writers worry that their initial effort isn't good enough. However, it's important to remember that a first draft is just that first attempt. With time, effort, and feedback, you can refine your work and turn it into something truly great. So, take a deep breath, celebrate your progress, and get ready to take the next step on your writing journey.

STEP 15 – DO YOUR FIRST EDIT / PROOF READ

Proofreading your novel's first draft is an important step in the writing process to catch errors, improve clarity, and polish your work. Here are some tips to help you self-proofread effectively:

Take a Break: After completing your first draft, step away from your novel for a while. This will allow you to approach it with fresh eyes and a more critical perspective.

Read Aloud: Read your novel out loud. This can help you catch awkward phrasing, pacing issues, and grammatical errors. It also makes it easier to spot inconsistencies and hear how the dialogue flows.

Edit for Grammar and Punctuation: Pay close attention to grammar, punctuation, and style. Ensure consistency in formatting (e.g., quotation marks, italics, capitalization). Check for subject-verb agreement, proper use of tenses, and common grammatical mistakes.

Focus on Clarity: Make sure your writing is clear and concise. Eliminate wordiness, jargon, and overly complex sentences. Ensure your writing flows logically and is easy for readers to understand.

Check for Consistency: Review character names, settings, and plot details for consistency throughout the novel. Ensure that your characters' traits, motivations, and relationships remain consistent.

Look for Repetition: Avoid repeating the same words or phrases too frequently. Use synonyms or rephrase sentences to maintain variety and engage the reader.

Watch for Typos and Spelling Errors: Carefully check for typos and spelling mistakes. Be mindful of commonly confused words and homophones, such as "their" and "there."

Examine Dialogue: Ensure that dialogue is realistic and engaging. Each character's voice should be distinct, and conversations should advance the plot or reveal character traits.

Check for Formatting and Layout: Make sure your manuscript is properly formatted with consistent font and paragraph spacing. Check for any layout or formatting issues that may disrupt the reading experience.

Edit in Passes: Instead of trying to tackle everything at once, focus on specific aspects in each pass. For example, in one pass, concentrate on grammar and punctuation, and in another pass, focus on character consistency.

Proofread Multiple Times: Don't expect to catch everything in one pass. Plan to proofread your novel multiple times, ideally with a specific focus for each round.

Remember that self-proofreading is a crucial part of the writing process, but it's not a substitute for professional editing. Even after you've self-proofread your novel, consider having it professionally edited to ensure the highest quality before publication.

STEP 16 – RESEARCH GRAMMAR CHECKERS

Using tools like **Grammarly** www.grammarly.com and **ProWritingAid** www.prowritingaid.com can greatly enhance the editing process for authors. These advanced writing assistance tools offer a multitude of benefits. Firstly, they provide comprehensive grammar and spelling checks, ensuring that your manuscript is free from common errors that can distract readers. Additionally, they offer style suggestions, helping to refine your prose for clarity and coherence. These tools also assist in detecting issues with punctuation, sentence structure, and word choice, contributing to a polished final product. Moreover, they offer valuable insights into readability and tone, allowing authors to fine-tune their writing to suit their target audience. Overall, incorporating these tools into the editing process can significantly streamline the revision process and elevate the overall quality of your book.

RESOURCES

Some alternatives are:

Hemingway Editor:
Provides feedback on sentence structure, readability, and suggests improvements for clarity and conciseness.
Website: www.hemingwayapp.com

Ginger:
Offers grammar and spelling checking, as well as a sentence rephrasing tool to improve writing style.
Website: www.gingersoftware.com

WhiteSmoke:
Offers grammar and punctuation checking, as well as style suggestions for better writing.
Website: www.whitesmoke.com

LanguageTool:
Provides grammar, style, and spell-checking in multiple languages.
Website: www.languagetool.org

Scribens:
Offers grammar and spelling checks, along with style suggestions to improve overall writing quality.
Website: www.scribens.com

Autocrit:
Designed specifically for fiction writers, Autocrit helps identify common issues in manuscripts such as pacing, dialogue, and more.
Website: www.autocrit.com

Reverso:
Offers grammar, spelling, and translation services, along with context-based corrections.
Website: www.reverso.net

PaperRater:
Provides grammar checking, plagiarism detection, and style suggestions.
Website: www.paperrater.com

Writer's Diet:
Focuses on identifying "flabby" or unnecessary words in your

writing to improve clarity and conciseness.
Website: www.writersdiet.com

After the Deadline:
Offers grammar, spelling, and style checking for web-based applications, including WordPress.
Website: www.afterthedeadline.com

Slick Write:
Provides real-time grammar checking, style suggestions, and detailed statistics about your writing.
Website: www.slickwrite.com

GrammarCheck:
Offers basic grammar and punctuation checking, along with style suggestions.
Website: www.grammarcheck.net

STEP 17 – USING EITHER GRAMMARLY OR PRO WRITING AID

Grammarly and ProWritingAid are both valuable tools for writers, especially when working on your first book. They can help you improve grammar, punctuation, style, and overall writing quality. Here's how to use these tools effectively:

Sign Up and Install the Tools:
Go to the Grammarly and ProWritingAid websites and sign up for an account.
Download and install the browser extension for both Grammarly and ProWritingAid. This will allow you to check your writing in various online platforms, including email, social media, and writing software.

Copy and Paste Your Text:
If you're using a word processing software like Microsoft Word, you can copy and paste your text directly into Grammarly or ProWritingAid's web editor.

Use the Browser Extensions:
As you write in your preferred word processing software (e.g., Microsoft Word, Google Docs), the Grammarly and ProWritingAid browser extensions will automatically check your text and provide suggestions in real-time. They will underline or highlight errors and offer suggestions for corrections.

Review and Accept Suggestions:

For each suggestion, carefully review it and decide whether it's appropriate for your writing. Grammarly and ProWritingAid will provide explanations and examples for most suggestions, helping you understand the issues.

Address Style and Clarity:
Both tools offer more than just grammar and spelling checks. They can help you improve the clarity, style, and overall quality of your writing. Consider their suggestions for sentence structure, word choice, and writing style.

Use the Desktop Apps:
Grammarly and ProWritingAid also offer desktop applications. You can copy and paste or import your text into these apps for a more comprehensive analysis of your writing. They provide detailed reports on various aspects of your text.

Work on Chapters or Sections:
Instead of checking your entire book at once, work on one chapter or section at a time. This makes the editing process more manageable and focused.

Save Your Progress:
Always make sure to save your progress as you work, especially if you're using the web-based editors. There's usually an option to save your documents in your Grammarly or ProWritingAid account.

Address Repeated Mistakes:
Pay attention to recurring mistakes highlighted by these tools. If you find you're making the same errors consistently, use these tools as a learning opportunity to improve your writing skills.

Seek a Second Opinion:
While Grammarly and ProWritingAid are powerful, they may not catch every issue or provide the context that a human editor can. Consider having a professional editor review your entire book for a final polish.

Keep Your Writing Voice:
Be cautious not to over-edit and lose your unique writing voice. Use the tools to enhance your writing but remember that it's essential to maintain your style and authenticity.

Save Versions:
Before making major revisions based on the tools' suggestions, consider saving a version of your book with those revisions and another without. This way, you can compare them and ensure the changes enhance your work.

Remember that while Grammarly and ProWritingAid are helpful, they are not a substitute for a human editor, especially when it comes to assessing the overall flow, plot, and character development in your book. Using these tools in combination with human editing can help you produce the best possible manuscript for your first book.

STEP 18 – CONSIDER USING A PROOF-READER

Benefits of Using a Proof-reader

Engaging the services of a professional proof-reader can be a pivotal step in the process of refining and perfecting your written work. Here are some of the key benefits of having a proof-reader:

Error-Free Content:
One of the primary advantages of hiring a proof-reader is the assurance of error-free content. A skilled proof-reader meticulously reviews your text, catching and rectifying grammar, spelling, and punctuation mistakes that may have been overlooked during the writing process. This results in a polished and professional final product.

Enhanced Clarity and Coherence:
Proof-readers have a keen eye for clarity and coherence. They identify and rectify issues with sentence structure, word choice, and overall flow, ensuring that your message is conveyed in the most effective and understandable way possible. This not only elevates the readability of your work but also enhances its impact on the reader.

Maintaining Professionalism and Credibility:
Presenting error-free, well-edited content is essential for maintaining professionalism and credibility, whether it's a business document, academic paper, or creative work. A proof-reader's expertise helps instil confidence in your audience, showcasing your commitment to quality and attention to detail.

Time and Effort Savings:
Hiring a proof-reader allows you to focus on your strengths and areas of expertise, rather than spending valuable time combing through your own work for errors. This frees up your time for other critical tasks, such as research, content creation, or strategic planning.

Objective Perspective:
A proof-reader brings an objective viewpoint to your work. They approach the text with fresh eyes, which can be invaluable in identifying and rectifying inconsistencies, ambiguities, or areas that may require clarification. This ensures that your message is conveyed accurately and effectively.

Adherence to Style Guides and Guidelines:
Depending on the context of your writing, there may be specific style guides or industry-specific guidelines that need to be followed. A skilled proof-reader is well-versed in various style conventions (such as APA, MLA, Chicago, etc.) and ensures that your work adheres to these standards.

Customized Feedback and Suggestions:
Beyond rectifying errors, a proof-reader provides valuable feedback and suggestions for improvement. They may offer insights on refining your writing style, optimizing sentence structure, or enhancing the overall impact of your content.

While hiring a proof-reader can offer many benefits, there are also some potential downsides to consider:

Cost:
Hiring a professional proof-reader can be an added expense, particularly for individuals or smaller organizations with limited budgets. The cost of proofreading services can vary depending on factors like the length and complexity of the document.

Dependence on External Help:
Relying on a proof-reader may lead to a dependency on external

assistance. This can potentially hinder the development of one's own proofreading and editing skills. It's important for authors to continue honing their own editing abilities.

Time Constraints:
Engaging a proof-reader may introduce additional time constraints. Waiting for the proof-reader to review and return the document can extend the overall timeline of a project, which may not be conducive to tight deadlines.

Loss of Personal Touch:
While a proof-reader's objective perspective is valuable, there's a risk of losing some of the author's personal style and voice in the process. Over-reliance on a proof-reader could potentially dilute the uniqueness of the author's writing.

Communication Challenges:
Misinterpretation of the author's intent or style can occur, especially if there is limited communication or understanding between the author and the proof-reader. This can lead to potential revisions that may not align with the author's vision.

Potential for Overediting:
In some cases, a proof-reader might be overly meticulous, making numerous changes that may not necessarily enhance the original content. This can sometimes result in a loss of the author's original voice and style.

Confidentiality Concerns:
Depending on the content being proofread, there may be concerns about confidentiality. It's important to ensure that the proof-reader is trustworthy and will handle sensitive information appropriately.

Availability and Reliability:
Depending on the proof-reader's workload and availability, there may be delays in getting the work completed. Additionally, if the

proof-reader is not reliable or fails to meet deadlines, it can cause disruptions to the author's schedule.

It's important for authors to weigh these potential downsides against the benefits of hiring a proof-reader. In some cases, the advantages of professional proofreading may far outweigh any potential drawbacks. Authors should carefully consider their specific needs, budget, and timeline before deciding whether to hire a proof-reader.

In conclusion, employing a professional proof-reader is a strategic investment in the quality and effectiveness of your written work. Their expertise not only results in a polished, error-free / near to error-free final product but also contributes to the overall professionalism and impact of your writing. Whether it's a business document, academic paper, or creative piece, a proof-reader plays a crucial role in ensuring that your work is presented at its absolute best.

STEP 19 – RESEARCH WAYS TO MAKE A BOOK COVER

Creating a book cover can be a fun and creative process. Here are several ways you can make a cover for your book:

Design Software: Use professional design software like Adobe Photoshop, Illustrator, or InDesign if you have the skills and access to these tools. They provide the most flexibility in design.

Online Design Tools: There are several online design tools that are user-friendly and don't require extensive design experience. Canva and Adobe Spark are popular options. They offer pre-made templates for book covers, making it easier to create a polished design.

Hire a Professional Designer: If you're not confident in your design skills or want a high-quality cover, consider hiring a professional book cover designer. They can bring your vision to life and ensure the cover looks appealing and marketable.

DIY with Image Editing Software: If you have some experience with image editing software like GIMP, Affinity, Pixlr, or even Microsoft Word, you can create a simple book cover by combining images, text, and basic design elements.

Stock Photos and Images: Purchase or use royalty-free stock photos and images that fit your book's theme. Many websites offer a wide variety of images you can use for a fee or for free, depending on the licensing terms.

Artwork or Illustrations: If you're an artist or know one, you can create custom artwork or illustrations for your book cover. Hand-drawn or digitally created illustrations can give your book a unique and personal touch.

Photography: Take your own photographs that are relevant to your book's content. High-quality personal photos can be an excellent choice for a book cover.

Typography: Experiment with different fonts and typography styles to create an attractive title and author name on the cover. Typography alone can make a striking book cover.

Templates: Some print-on-demand and self-publishing platforms, like Amazon Kindle Direct Publishing, provide cover templates to help you design a cover that fits their specifications.

Feedback and Testing: Once you have a design, seek feedback from friends, colleagues, or potential readers. It's essential to get multiple opinions to ensure your cover is appealing and conveys the right message.

STEP 20 – STUDY SUCCESSFUL BOOK COVERS

What makes a successful book cover?

A successful book cover is a crucial element in attracting potential readers and conveying the essence of the book. Here are key factors that contribute to a successful book cover:

Visual Appeal: The cover should be visually appealing, grabbing the viewer's attention and piquing their interest. Eye-catching colours, striking images or illustrations, and well-chosen typography play a significant role in drawing readers in.

Relevance to Content: The cover should accurately reflect the content, genre, and themes of the book. It should give readers a sense of what to expect inside, ensuring that it aligns with their interests and expectations.

Clear Design: Clarity is crucial. The cover design should be uncluttered and easy to understand at a glance. It should convey the book's message or genre without causing confusion or overwhelming the viewer.

Professional Quality: The cover design should look professionally crafted. Amateurish or poorly executed designs can give the impression of low-quality content inside, potentially turning potential readers away.

Typography and Font Choice: The font used for the title and author name should be legible, appropriate for the genre, and complement the overall design. It should also be readable in different sizes, from thumbnail to full size.

Balance and Composition: A successful cover maintains a balanced composition, with elements (title, images, author name, etc.) arranged in a visually pleasing and harmonious manner. The layout should guide the viewer's eye smoothly across the cover.

Unique Branding: A cover can contribute to an author's or a series' brand identity. If it's part of a series, there should be consistent elements (such as font, colour scheme, or imagery) that tie it to other books in the series.

Emotional Connection: The cover should evoke an emotional response or intrigue the viewer, creating a connection that compels them to explore further. It should resonate with the target audience's sensibilities and interests.

Standout Thumbnail: In an era of online shopping and e-books, a successful cover must also be effective as a small thumbnail image. It should remain clear and compelling even at reduced sizes.

Market Research and Audience Alignment: The cover design should consider the preferences and expectations of the target audience. Understanding what resonates with potential readers in the book's genre is crucial.
Versatility:

If the book will be published in various formats (print, e-book, audiobook), the cover design should be adaptable to different dimensions and orientations while maintaining its impact.

Legally Compliant: The cover should not infringe on copyright laws, ensuring that all images, fonts, and elements used are properly licensed or royalty-free.
A successful book cover serves as a powerful marketing tool, enticing readers to pick up the book and explore its contents. It is a visual representation of the author's work, making it crucial to invest time and resources into creating a cover that effectively

captures the essence of the book.

Research book covers

Studying successful book covers can provide valuable insights into what makes a cover visually appealing and effective in attracting readers. Here are some steps you can take to study successful book covers:

Visit Bookstores: Go to physical bookstores or browse online retailers to see a wide range of book covers in different genres. Pay attention to bestsellers and books that catch your eye. Take notes or photographs of covers that stand out.

Analyse Design Elements: Break down the design elements of successful book covers. This includes the use of colour, typography, imagery, layout, and overall composition. Consider how these elements work together to create a visually appealing cover.

Identify Trends: Look for design trends within specific genres. Different genres often have common visual themes and styles. Analyse how successful books within a genre follow or subvert these trends to stand out.

Research Online: Use websites, blogs, and social media platforms dedicated to book cover design and analysis. These sources often discuss the latest trends and showcase successful covers. Goodreads and book-related forums are also great places to find discussions about book covers.

Read Design Books: There are books and resources dedicated to the art and science of book cover design. Some notable ones include "The Anatomy of a Book Cover" by Nigel Salter and "The Book Cover in the Weimar Republic" by Jamie H. Trnka.

Follow Designers and Publishers: Follow book cover designers, illustrators, and publishing houses on social media platforms like Instagram and Pinterest.

Online Marketplaces: Websites like Amazon, Goodreads, and BookBub often allow you to explore books by category or genre, making it easy to examine bestsellers and their covers in a particular niche.

Art and Design Exhibitions: Attend art and design exhibitions in your area. These events often feature book cover design as an art form, and you can gain inspiration from a broader design perspective.

Create a Mood Board: Collect images of book covers that resonate with you and create a mood board. This can help you identify common elements and aesthetics that you find appealing.

Get Feedback: Share your observations with others, especially people who are your target audience. Ask for their opinions on what elements they find appealing and why.

Experiment and Practice: Once you've learned from successful book covers, try applying what you've discovered to your own designs. Experiment with different combinations of elements and keep refining your skills.

Remember that while studying successful book covers is valuable, it's also important to make your cover unique and reflective of your book's content and style. What works for one book may not work for another, so adapt your findings to fit the specific needs of your project.

STEP 21 – TIME TO MAKE YOUR BOOK COVER

Armed with the tools and knowledge it is now time to design your book cover. If this is something that really falls outside of your skillset or something that you feel comfortable with then there is support out there.

RESOURCES

A list of companies that can provide cover design for you are listed below. Please however be careful of who you choose and try and establish the terms for stage payments or payment on completion and signoff so that you do not get ripped off.

99designs:

- Website: www.99designs.com

  Description: 99designs is a platform that connects authors with a community of freelance designers who can create custom book covers. Authors can run design contests or work directly with a designer.

Reedsy:

- Website: www.reedsy.com
- Description: Reedsy is a marketplace that connects authors with professional freelancers, including book cover designers. They carefully vet their designers to ensure high quality.

Meet The Authors:

- Website: www.meettheauthors.net
- Description: Meet The Authors is a platform where authors can connect with a community of professionals, including book cover designers. It provides a platform for authors to showcase their work and find services related to book publishing.

Damonza:

- Website: www.damonza.com
- Description: Damonza specialises in book cover design and offers a range of packages to fit different budgets. They have a portfolio showcasing their past work.

The Book Cover Designer:

- Website: www.thebookcoverdesigner.com
- Description: This website is a marketplace for pre-made book covers, where authors can purchase existing designs. They also offer custom design services.

CrowdSpring:

- Website: www.crowdspring.com
- Description: CrowdSpring is a platform that allows authors to run design contests for various projects, including book covers. Designers from around the world can submit their concepts.

Fiverr:

- Website: www.fiverr.com
- Description: Fiverr is a popular freelance marketplace where you can find a wide range of services, including book cover design. You can browse through profiles of individual designers and choose the one that fits your style and budget.

STEP 22 – DOWNLOAD BOOK TEMPLATES

Choosing the right book template size is a crucial step in the publishing process as it affects how the book is perceived by readers and distributed in the market. The size should align with the genre, content, and target audience of the book. For example, fiction novels typically come in standard sizes like 5.5 x 8.5 inches or 6 x 9 inches. These sizes strike a balance between portability and readability, making them popular choices for most fiction genres. On the other hand, larger sizes like 8.5 x 11 inches are more common for coffee table books, art books, and children's picture books, where the visuals play a significant role in the reader's experience. These larger sizes allow for more expansive layouts and vivid imagery.

Consider the content and purpose of your book when choosing the template size. For example, a pocket-sized guidebook or travel manual may benefit from a smaller format, making it easy for readers to carry around. Alternatively, a cookbook with detailed recipes and images might opt for a larger, more spacious format to showcase the visuals and allow for easy reference. Additionally, consider industry standards and reader expectations. Readers often have certain size expectations based on the genre and format of a book. Straying too far from these norms can impact how your book is received. Ultimately, the right book template size should enhance the reading experience and complement the content and style of your book.

Several self-publishing platforms provide downloadable book templates to help you format your book for publishing. These templates are typically available in various formats, including Microsoft Word, InDesign, and other software commonly used for book layout.

RESOURCES

Here are a few self-publishing sites that offer book templates:

Amazon Kindle Direct Publishing (KDP): KDP provides free downloadable templates for paperback and Kindle eBook formatting. These templates help ensure your book meets Amazon's publishing guidelines.

Blurb: Blurb offers a variety of book-making tools, including downloadable templates for both print and e-book projects. They have templates for various book sizes and styles.

Lulu: Lulu provides free downloadable templates for various book sizes and formats. These templates are available for both print and e-book publishing.

BookBaby: BookBaby offers free downloadable templates for book layout and cover design. They provide templates for both print and e-book formats.

CreateSpace (now part of KDP): While CreateSpace has merged with Amazon KDP, some resources, and templates from the CreateSpace platform are still accessible through KDP. You can find book templates there as well.

IngramSpark: IngramSpark offers downloadable book templates for various trim sizes and types of books. They provide templates for both print and e-book publishing.

Reedsy: Reedsy provides a free online tool called the Reedsy Book Editor, which allows you to create and format your book. While it's not a downloadable template, it's a user-friendly online tool for book formatting.

BookWright (by Blurb): If you're using Blurb to publish your book, they offer the BookWright software, which allows you to create and format your book with a user-friendly interface.

When using these templates, make sure to follow the specific guidelines and instructions provided by each platform to ensure your book's interior and cover meet their requirements. Additionally, it's a good practice to review your book carefully after formatting to check for any layout or design issues before publishing.

STEP 23 – CREATING A PUBLISHING PLAN

1. Pre-Launch Preparation:
Define Your Target Audience: Clearly identify the demographic and interests of your ideal readers. Tailor your marketing efforts to resonate with this audience.

Build an Author Platform: Establish a strong online presence through social media, a professional website, and author profiles on platforms like Goodreads. Engage with potential readers and create a community around your book.

Craft a Compelling Book Description: Create an enticing book description that highlights the key themes, characters, and unique selling points of your book. This will be crucial for online retailers and promotional materials.

2. Professional Editing and Cover Design:
Editing: As we have mentioned previously, invest in professional editing services to ensure your manuscript is polished and error-free. A well-edited book is more likely to receive positive reviews and word-of-mouth recommendations.

Cover Design: Create an eye-catching and genre-appropriate book cover. A visually appealing cover is a powerful marketing tool and can significantly impact sales.

3. Distribution Strategy:
Choose Publishing Platforms: Decide whether you'll pursue traditional publishing, self-publishing, or a hybrid approach. Research and select the most suitable publishing platforms for

your book.

Format Options: Consider releasing your book in various formats, including e-book, paperback, and audiobook. Catering to different reader preferences can broaden your audience.

4. Marketing and Promotion:
Create a Marketing Timeline: Develop a timeline outlining pre-launch, launch, and post-launch marketing activities. This should include social media campaigns, email marketing, and any paid advertising efforts.

Leverage Book Reviews: Secure early reviews from beta readers, influencers, and reputable book reviewers. Positive reviews can boost credibility and attract more readers.

Book Launch Event: Plan a virtual or physical launch event to generate excitement around your book. Consider collaborations with other authors, influencers, or book clubs.

5. Post-Launch Engagement:
Sustain Marketing Efforts: Keep the momentum going post-launch with ongoing marketing activities. Explore promotions, discounts, or limited time offers to maintain interest.

Author Interviews and Features: Seek opportunities for author interviews, guest blog posts, and features on relevant podcasts or media outlets. This helps to keep your book in the spotlight.

Engage with Readers: Actively engage with readers through social media, book clubs, and author Q&A sessions. Building a connection with your audience can lead to long-term success.

6. Monitor and Adapt:
Track Sales and Analytics: Regularly monitor sales data, reader reviews, and other analytics to assess the effectiveness of your marketing strategies. Adjust your plan based on the insights gained.

Iterate Your Marketing Plan: Stay flexible and be willing to iterate your marketing plan based on what works best for your book and audience. Experiment with new promotional activities to discover additional opportunities.

By carefully considering these elements and tailoring your plan to fit the specific characteristics of your book and target audience, you'll be well-positioned to navigate the complexities of book publishing and increase the chances of a successful launch.

STEP 24 – LEARN HOW TO PUBLISH ON AMAZON KDP

Amazon Kindle Direct Publishing (KDP) is a platform that empowers authors and independent publishers to bring their written works to a global audience in digital and print formats. Launched by Amazon, KDP has revolutionized the publishing industry by offering a straightforward and accessible means for authors to self-publish their books. Here's a breakdown of what Amazon KDP is and how it works:

1. Self-Publishing Platform:

Amazon KDP serves as a self-publishing platform, enabling authors to independently publish and distribute their e-books and paperbacks. This eliminates the need for traditional publishing houses, giving authors direct control over their creative work and its dissemination.

2. E-Book and Paperback Publishing:

E-Books: Authors can format and upload their manuscripts as e-books, reaching Kindle readers worldwide. This digital format allows for easy accessibility on Kindle devices, as well as through Kindle apps on smartphones, tablets, and computers.

Paperbacks: In addition to e-books, KDP supports the creation and distribution of paperback versions of books. This provides authors with the opportunity to offer physical copies to readers who prefer the tactile experience of a printed book.

3. Global Distribution:

Amazon Kindle Store: Once published on KDP, books become available for purchase on the Amazon Kindle Store, reaching a vast global audience. Readers can easily discover, purchase, and download e-books to their devices.

Expanded Distribution: Authors can also opt for expanded distribution to make their paperback books available to a wider network of online retailers, bookstores, and academic institutions.

4. Royalty Options:

Amazon KDP offers flexible royalty options, allowing authors to choose between two primary models:

70% Royalty: Authors can earn a 70% royalty on e-books sold in certain markets, provided pricing and distribution criteria are met.

35% Royalty: For books priced outside the criteria for the 70% option or in specific markets, a 35% royalty rate applies.

5. User-Friendly Interface:

Book Management Dashboard: Authors have access to a user-friendly dashboard where they can manage their book details, pricing, and distribution settings. This interface simplifies the process of updating and monitoring book listings.

6. Promotional Tools:

Kindle Countdown Deals and Free Book Promotions: KDP offers promotional tools such as Kindle Countdown Deals and Free Book Promotions, allowing authors to temporarily discount or offer their e-books for free to boost visibility and attract readers.

7. Real-Time Reporting:

Authors can track their sales, monitor royalties, and gain insights into reader engagement through KDP's real-time reporting features. This data helps authors make informed decisions about marketing and promotional strategies.

In essence, Amazon KDP provides authors with a powerful and accessible platform to publish, distribute, and promote their books globally, democratizing the publishing process and allowing diverse voices to reach a wide audience with ease.

STEP 25 – CONSIDER USING A PUBLISHING SERVICE

Navigating Publishing Options: Factors to Consider and Support Resources

Publishing a book involves critical decisions about the path to publication, and authors often face the choice between traditional publishing, self-publishing, or utilizing assisted publishing services. Here are key considerations and some support organizations to aid in this decision-making process:

1. Traditional Publishing vs. Self-Publishing:

Traditional Publishing:

Advantages: Prestige, wider distribution, editorial and marketing support.

Considerations: Often involves querying literary agents, lengthy submission processes, and giving up some creative control.

Self-Publishing:

Advantages: Creative control, faster time to market, higher royalty rates.

Considerations: Responsibility for editing, cover design, and marketing falls on the author; potential challenges in distribution and visibility.

2. Assisted Publishing Services:

Vanity Publishing:

Features: Authors pay for the entire publishing process, including editing, cover design, and distribution.

Considerations: Costly; some may provide quality services, while others might exploit authors.

RESOURCES

Other Companies to Consider:

BookBaby: Provides a comprehensive suite of publishing services, including editing, design, and distribution. Authors can choose specific services based on their needs.

Meet the Authors: Offers support with manuscript assessment, editing, publishing and marketing.

Reedsy: Connects authors with professional editors, designers, and marketers. It allows for a more tailored approach by letting authors assemble their own publishing team.

Draft2Digital: Simplifies the self-publishing process by offering formatting, distribution, and promotional tools. It's known for its user-friendly interface.

STEP 26 – PUBLISH PAPERBACK ON AMAZON

Congratulations! You are now at the point of Publishing a paper back on Amazon Kindle Direct Publishing (KDP). Here's a quick step-by-step guide to help you navigate the process:

Step 1: Double check your Manuscript
Before you jump into the publishing process, make sure your manuscript is polished and formatted correctly. Double-check for grammar and spelling errors as explained previously. Ensure that your book cover is visually appealing and professional.

Step 2: Create an Amazon KDP Account
If you don't already have an Amazon KDP account, go to the KDP website, and sign up. You'll need to provide some basic information, including your name, address, and banking details for royalty payments.

Step 3: Add a New Paperback Title
Once logged into your KDP account, click on the "Create a Paperback" button. You'll be prompted to fill in details such as the book title, author name, description, and keywords. Be sure to choose the appropriate categories and add any necessary contributors.

Step 4: Upload Your Manuscript
Follow the instructions to upload your formatted manuscript. Amazon provides guidelines for formatting, including accepted file types (e.g., PDF, DOC, or DOCX). Ensure that your manuscript meets these requirements for a smooth upload.

Step 5: Design Your Cover

Use Amazon's cover creator or upload your previously designed cover.

Step 6: Set Your Paperback Pricing
Determine the pricing for your paperback. Consider factors like production cost, royalty rates, and competitive pricing in your genre. Amazon will provide a minimum and maximum price based on the book's specifications.

Step 7: Choose Distribution Channels
Decide where you want your book to be available. You can choose to distribute it globally through Amazon's expanded distribution network or limit it to specific regions.

Step 8: Enrol in KDP Select (Optional)
KDP Select is a program that allows you to make your book exclusive to Kindle for a specific period. This decision depends on your marketing strategy and goals.

Step 9: Review and Publish
Carefully review all the details you've entered, preview your book, and make any necessary changes. Once you're satisfied, click the "Publish Your Paperback Book" button.

Be aware that it can take 24 hours for your book to be approved and published onto Amazon.

STEP 27 – ORDER YOUR AUTHOR COPIES

Ordering author copies of your paperback book on Amazon Kindle Direct Publishing (KDP) is a convenient way to receive physical copies of your own book for personal use or for promotional purposes. Here's how to order author copies on Amazon KDP:

Log into Your KDP Account:

Visit the KDP website (https://kdp.amazon.com/) and log in with your KDP account credentials.

Access Your Paperback Book:

On your KDP dashboard, click on the book title for which you want to order author copies. This will take you to the book's details page.

Navigate to "Paperback Rights & Pricing":

n the "Paperback Rights & Pricing" section, you'll find an option for "Author Copies." Click on "Order Author Copies."

Choose the Quantity:

Select the quantity of author copies you'd like to order. You can order a specific number of copies, but there may be a minimum or maximum limit depending on the book's trim size, page count, and other factors.

Review and Confirm Details:

Review the details of your order, including the estimated cost, shipping address, and payment method. Ensure that all information is accurate before proceeding.

Place Your Order:

Once you're satisfied with the order details, click the "Submit Order" or "Place Your Order" button. You may need to provide payment information at this point if you haven't already.

Review Shipping and Payment Information:

Check and confirm the shipping address and payment method for your order. You'll see the estimated delivery date for your author copies.

Complete the Order:

Click the "Place Your Order" or "Complete Order" button to finalize the purchase. Amazon KDP will process your order and provide you with an order confirmation.

Track Your Order:

You can track the status of your order through your KDP account. You'll receive updates on the order's progress, including when it's shipped and when you can expect to receive it.

Receive Your Author Copies:

Once your author copies are printed and shipped, they will be delivered to the shipping address you specified during the order process. The delivery time may vary depending on your location.

Author copies are typically printed and shipped from Amazon facilities, and you will be charged for the cost of the copies and shipping. The prices may vary based on factors like the book's trim size, page count, and location of delivery. Keep in mind that you'll also have to pay for any applicable taxes and shipping fees.

Ordering author copies through KDP is a convenient way to

obtain physical copies of your book for various purposes, such as giveaways, signings, or personal use.

STEP 28 – FINAL PROOFREAD AND EDIT USING YOUR PAPERBACK

This is an incredibly exciting and rewarding part of the process.

You have laboured long and hard and put so much of yourself into this piece of work. If this is your first time, you will have realised that writing is therapeutic, cathartic and is an extension of yourself but as a self-published author you must learn how to do all the other stuff unless you enlist help.

Unwrapping your first ever book is quite wonderful even if it's not perfect yet. In fact, I think we would both be very surprised, if at this stage, everything was perfect.

You will find that your book seems very different once it has been transformed into something you can hold in your hand.

I have learnt that every time I do this, I can enjoy the story in its entirety, understand if there are any holes in it and whether it's entertaining. But more importantly, typos and other mistakes tend to jump out at you.

The method I use is simply to mark the errors in pencil and then write the page number either on another piece of paper or in the back of the book. When you return to your original script, you just need to reference those to make changes to both your paperback and your e-book.

STEP 29 – PUBLISH AS AN EBOOK ON AMAZON

Publishing an eBook on Amazon Kindle Direct Publishing (KDP) is a straightforward process. Here's a step-by-step guide to help you get started:

Step 1: Create an Amazon KDP Account
If you don't already have an account, go to the Amazon KDP website, and sign up. Provide the necessary information, including your name, address, and banking details for royalty payments.

Step 2: Add a New Kindle eBook Title
Once logged into your KDP account, click on the "Create a Kindle eBook" button. Fill in the required details, such as the book title, author name, description, and keywords. Choose the appropriate categories and add contributors if needed.

Step 3: Upload Your Manuscript
Prepare your eBook manuscript in a supported format (e.g., MOBI, EPUB). Follow Amazon's formatting guidelines to ensure a smooth upload. You can preview your eBook before publishing to catch any formatting issues.

Step 4: Add your Book Cover
Add your book cover. Be aware that this may be different to the one you have created for your paperback.

Step 5: Set Your eBook Pricing
Determine the pricing for your eBook. Consider factors like genre, competition, and your marketing strategy. Amazon provides

options for royalty rates based on your pricing choices.

Step 6: Enrol in KDP Select (Optional)
Decide whether to enrol your eBook in KDP Select, a program that allows Amazon to be the exclusive distributor of your eBook for a specific period. This can impact promotions and reach.

Step 7: Preview Your e-Book
Before publishing, use the online previewer to check how your eBook will appear on Kindle devices. Make sure page breaks fall in the correct place and make any necessary adjustments to formatting or layout.

Step 8: Publish Your e-Book
Once you're satisfied with all the details, click the "Publish Your Kindle eBook" button. Your eBook will be available on Amazon within 72 hours. You can make updates or changes even after publishing.

STEP 30 – RESEARCH APPLE BOOKS

Apple Books is Apple's digital reading platform, offering a diverse and extensive collection of eBooks for users of Apple devices. Here's our overview of Apple Books:

1. Access and Compatibility:

Apple Books is accessible on Apple devices, including iPhones, iPads, Macs, and iPod Touch.

Users can access their purchased books across devices through iCloud synchronization.

2. Bookstore and Selection:

The Apple Books Store is a digital marketplace where users can browse, purchase, and download eBooks.

The store features a vast selection of eBooks, audiobooks, and textbooks across various genres, catering to a broad range of reader preferences.

3. User Interface and Reading Experience:

The Apple Books app provides a user-friendly interface with features like a customizable reading experience, including font adjustments, background colours, and brightness controls.

Users can organize their library, create custom bookshelves, and use bookmarks and annotations for a personalized reading experience.

4. Multi-Format Support:

Apple Books supports various eBook formats, including EPUB and PDF, making it compatible with a wide range of digital publications.

5. Audiobooks and Enhanced eBooks:

In addition to traditional eBooks, Apple Books offers a substantial collection of audiobooks.

Some eBooks on Apple Books may include enhanced features like multimedia elements, interactive content, and author interviews.

6. Pricing and Purchasing:

Users can purchase books directly from the Apple Books Store using their Apple ID.

Pricing is determined by the publishers, and users can find a mix of free, discounted, and full-priced eBooks.

7. Sync Across Devices:

Apple Books utilises iCloud to sync the user's library, bookmarks, and annotations across all their Apple devices seamlessly.

8. Self-Publishing through Apple Books:

Authors and independent publishers can use Apple Books for self-publishing through the Apple Books Author platform.

The platform provides tools for creating interactive eBooks and publishing directly to the Apple Books Store.

9. Privacy and Security:

Apple emphasizes user privacy and does not share personal reading data with third parties without user consent.

10. Education and Textbooks:

Apple Books is a common platform for educational content, including textbooks, providing features like interactive diagrams and multimedia elements.

11. Integration with Other Apple Services:

Apple Books integrates with other Apple services like Apple Music, Apple TV, and the Apple News app, creating a unified ecosystem for content consumption.

Certainly, advertising on Apple Books, like any platform, comes with its own set of advantages and disadvantages. Here are some pros and cons to consider:

Pros:

Apple Ecosystem Exposure:

Advertising on Apple Books provides exposure to a vast user base within the Apple ecosystem, including iPhone, iPad, and Mac users.

Quality Audience:

Apple device users often represent a demographic with higher purchasing power, potentially leading to a more financially attractive audience.

Interactive Content Options:

Apple Books supports interactive content, making it possible to create engaging and multimedia-rich advertisements.

Apple News Integration:

Advertising on Apple Books may extend your reach through integration with other Apple services like Apple News.

Global Reach:

Apple Books has a global presence, allowing you to target a diverse and international audience.

Cons:

Smaller Market Share:

While Apple's user base is substantial, it is smaller than that of other e-commerce giants like Amazon. This may limit the potential reach of your advertising efforts.

Limited Ad Formats:

As of my knowledge cut-off in early 2022, Apple Books had limited advertising options compared to other platforms. The available ad formats may not be as diverse or flexible as those on other platforms.

Cost:

Advertising costs on Apple Books might be relatively high, especially when compared to other digital advertising platforms.

Dependency on Apple Ecosystem:

Your advertising success is tied to the popularity and usage of Apple devices. If your target audience primarily uses non-Apple devices, the effectiveness of your campaign may be limited.

Competition:

Depending on your niche, the competition for advertising space on Apple Books can be intense, potentially driving up costs and making it challenging to stand out.

Limited Analytics:

Apple Books may provide limited analytics compared to other advertising platforms, making it harder to track the effectiveness of your campaigns.

Before deciding to advertise on Apple Books, it's essential to assess your target audience, advertising goals, and budget. Consider testing the platform with a smaller campaign to evaluate its effectiveness for your specific product or service.

In summary, Apple Books is a versatile and user-friendly platform that caters to readers across various genres and preferences. Whether you're into traditional eBooks, audiobooks, or interactive content, Apple Books provides a comprehensive reading experience within the Apple ecosystem.

STEP 31 – PUBLISH YOUR BOOK ON APPLE BOOKS

Publishing a book on Apple Books (formerly known as iBooks) involves several steps. Apple Books is a platform that allows authors to sell their e-books to a global audience. Here's a step-by-step guide on how to publish a book on Apple Books:

1. Prepare Your Manuscript:

Ensure your manuscript is properly formatted and edited.

Save your book in EPUB format, as this is the preferred format for Apple Books. EPUB is an open standard for e-books.

2. Set Up an Apple ID:

If you don't already have an Apple ID, you'll need to create one. Visit the Apple ID creation page (https://appleid.apple.com/) to sign up.

3. Get a Mac and Install macOS:

To publish on Apple Books, you need a Mac computer with macOS. Apple's iBooks Author and the Books for Authors app, which you'll use for the publishing process, are macOS applications.

4. Download and Install Books for Authors:

Download the Books for Authors app from the Mac App Store if you don't already have it installed. This application is essential for publishing on Apple Books.

5. Sign into Books for Authors:

Open the Books for Authors app and sign in with your Apple ID.

6. Create a New Book:

In the Books for Authors app, click on "Create a new book" to start the publishing process.

7. Enter Book Details:

Fill in information about your book, such as the title, author name, and description.

8. Import Your EPUB File:

You'll be prompted to import your EPUB file. This is where you'll upload your prepared manuscript.

9. Add Book Cover:

Design and upload a cover image for your book.

10. Set Price and Territories:

Specify the price of your book and select the territories where you want it to be available.

11. Choose Distribution Options:

Decide whether you want to distribute your book exclusively on Apple Books or through other platforms. Apple's Books app offers features like Apple Books Author, which can be useful for multimedia e-books.

12. Review and Publish:

Review all the information you've entered, including pricing and distribution options, and make sure everything is accurate.

13. Publish Your Book:

Once you are satisfied with your book's details, click the "Publish" button.

14. Review and Approval:

Apple Books will review your book before making it available to the public. This process may take several days, during which Apple will ensure that your book meets its standards and guidelines.

Remember that Apple Books, like other e-book platforms, requires you to adhere to their guidelines and standards. Ensuring that your manuscript and book details meet these requirements will help expedite the publishing process. Once your book is live on Apple Books, you can start reaching a global audience and potentially generate sales.

STEP 32 – RESEARCH INTO GOODREADS

Goodreads is a widely popular and influential platform designed for book enthusiasts and readers. Launched in 2007, it has grown to become one of the largest online communities dedicated to literature. Here's an overview of what Goodreads is all about:

1. Social Networking for Readers:

Community Hub: Goodreads acts as a social networking platform specifically tailored for bibliophiles. It brings together readers from around the world to share their love for books.

2. Personal Bookshelves:

Virtual Bookshelves: Users can create virtual bookshelves to organize and track the books they've read, want to read, and are currently reading. This feature helps users curate their literary preferences and keep a digital record of their reading journey.

3. Book Recommendations:

Personalized Recommendations: Goodreads provides personalized book recommendations based on users' reading history and preferences. This feature assists readers in discovering new books and authors aligned with their tastes.

4. Reading Challenges:

Setting Goals: Users can set yearly reading challenges, specifying the number of books they aim to read within a given timeframe. This feature encourages goal-setting and fosters a sense of accomplishment.

5. Book Reviews and Ratings:

User-Generated Reviews: Goodreads allows users to write and share reviews for books they've read. The platform also supports a five-star rating system, providing quick insights into the popularity of a book within the community.

6. Author Engagement:

Author Profiles: Authors can create profiles on Goodreads to connect with readers. This interaction often includes Q&A sessions, updates on upcoming releases, and the ability to respond to reader reviews.

7. Literary Events and Awards:

Bookish Events: Goodreads hosts literary events, including virtual book clubs, author interviews, and discussions. The platform also organizes the annual Goodreads Choice Awards, where users vote for their favourite books in various genres.

8. Book Lists and Genres:

Curated Lists: Users can explore curated book lists, categorized by genres, themes, and topics. These lists offer a wealth of recommendations and help users discover books they might have otherwise overlooked.

9. Integration with Other Platforms:

Connecting with Friends: Goodreads allows users to connect with friends, see what they are reading, and share book recommendations. The platform also integrates with other social media platforms.

10. Mobile App:

On-the-Go Access: Goodreads provides a mobile app for both iOS and Android devices, enabling users to access their bookshelves, write reviews, and engage with the community while on the go.

In essence, Goodreads is more than just a digital library; it's a dynamic and interactive space where readers can connect, explore new literary worlds, and share their passion for books with a global community of like-minded individuals. Whether you're an avid reader looking for your next favourite book or an author seeking to connect with your audience, Goodreads offers a vibrant and inclusive platform for all things literary.

STEP 33 – ADDING YOUR BOOK TO GOODREADS

Adding your book to Goodreads is a great way to increase its visibility among readers. Here's a step-by-step guide on how to add your book to Goodreads:

Step 1: Create a Goodreads Account
If you don't already have a Goodreads account, visit the Goodreads website (www.goodreads.com) and sign up. You can either sign up with an existing email account or use your Facebook account for a quick registration.

Step 2: Complete Your Goodreads Author Profile (For Authors)
If you're an author, claim your author profile on Goodreads. Search for your name on Goodreads, locate your author profile, and click on the "Is this you? Let us know!" link. Follow the instructions to verify your authorship.

Step 3: Search for Your Book
Once you're logged in, use the search bar at the top of the Goodreads homepage to find your book. Enter the title, author name, or ISBN to narrow down the search results.

Step 4: Navigate to the Book Listing
Locate your book in the search results and click on its title to go to the book's page.

Step 5: Add a New Book (If Not Already Listed)
If your book isn't already listed on Goodreads, you'll need to add it. On the book's page, look for the "Manually add a book" link (usually found at the bottom of the page) and click it.

Step 6: Fill in Book Details

If you're adding the book manually, you'll need to fill in various details such as the book title, author name, ISBN, publication date, and book cover. Provide accurate information to ensure your book is easily discoverable by readers.

Step 7: Set Your Book's Settings
Configure additional settings for your book, such as choosing the appropriate book edition, adding genres, and indicating whether the book is part of a series.

Step 8: Save Changes
After entering all the necessary information, click the "Save" or "Add Book" button to create your book listing.

Step 9: Edit Book Details (Optional)
You can further enhance your book listing by adding a book description, quotes, and additional details. Click on the "Edit Details" button on your book's page to make any modifications.

Step 10: Share Your Book
Encourage readers to add your book to their "Want to Read" shelf by sharing your Goodreads book link on your social media platforms, website, or through promotional materials.

Step 11: Engage with Readers
Respond to reviews, participate in discussions, and engage with readers who have added your book. Building a presence on Goodreads can help you connect with your audience.

Congratulations! Your book is now listed on Goodreads, and readers can discover and engage with it on this popular literary platform. Keep your Goodreads profile updated with any new releases or relevant information to maintain an active presence within the community.

STEP 34 – ADDING YOUR BOOK TO THE ASPA LIBRARY

As a valued member of ASPA, you are entitled to display your book in the ASPA Library. Our virtual storefront which links directly to you Amazon book sales page and Goodreads profile.

Adding your book to the ASPA library is easy and best of all free!

Simply click here to submit your book details or go to the members page where you will find a link within the ASPA library section. Alternatively we have placed a further link at the bottom of the library page.

You will be required to enter the following information:

- * Your Full Name
- * **Your Author Name / Pen Name** (It is quite common to not use your real name and to use a pen name instead)
- * **Your Email Address** (In case we have a question about your submission)
- **Your Phone Number**
- * **Book Title**
- * **Synopsis**
- * **Genre**
- * **Amazon URL**
- **Goodreads URL**
- **Part of a series or collection?** Yes / No
- **ISBN / ASIN** This will have been provided to you by Amazon if you haven't purchased your own

* = Required fields

Once you have provided us with this information we will check out the book on Amazon and collect the cover image before adding your book to the ASPA Library.

STEP 35 – CREATING YOUR ONLINE AUTHOR WEBSITE

Having an author website is a cornerstone of a successful author's online presence. It serves as the digital home where readers, fans, and industry professionals can gather to learn more about the author and their literary works. An author website offers a centralized platform for presenting a professional image, showcasing a comprehensive author bio, and highlighting a diverse portfolio of written works. Beyond a static biography, it becomes a dynamic space for engaging directly with the audience through blog posts, newsletters, and social media integration. The website acts as a powerful promotional tool, providing a visual gallery of book covers, synopses, and direct links for purchasing. This direct connection with readers fosters a sense of community and loyalty, creating a valuable space for author-branding, event promotion, and the dissemination of important updates. Ultimately, an author website is an indispensable tool for building an online identity, connecting with the audience, and establishing a lasting presence in the literary landscape.

Benefits of Having an Author Website:

Professional Presence:

An author website provides a professional and centralized online hub where readers, publishers, and the media can learn more about you and your work.

Author Branding:

Build and reinforce your author brand by showcasing your unique style, genre, and personality through a custom-designed website.

Direct Connection with Readers:

Engage directly with your readers through blog posts, newsletters, and social media integration, fostering a sense of community and loyalty.

Book Promotion:

Effectively promote your books by featuring book covers, synopses, and links to purchase or pre-order. This can significantly boost your book sales.

Author Bio and Portfolio:

Provide an in-depth author bio, showcase your writing portfolio, and highlight your achievements, creating a comprehensive overview for visitors.

Event Promotion:

Advertise book signings, speaking engagements, or virtual events on your website, keeping your audience informed and involved.

Newsletter Sign-Up:

Build a mailing list by incorporating a newsletter sign-up feature, allowing you to communicate directly with your readers and share updates.

Media and Press Kit:

Make it easy for journalists and media outlets to access essential information by including a press kit with high-resolution images, author interviews, and press releases.

Social Proof:

Display reader reviews, testimonials, and endorsements to establish credibility and influence potential readers.

Sell Merchandise:

If you have branded merchandise such as T-shirts or signed copies, an author website provides a platform to sell these items directly to your audience.

RESOURCES

Author Website Design Companies / Software:

Squarespace:

Squarespace offers visually appealing and user-friendly website templates suitable for authors. Their drag-and-drop interface makes customization straightforward.

Wix:

Wix is a versatile website builder with numerous templates and features. It's suitable for authors who want a customizable and visually engaging site.

WordPress (Self-Hosted):

WordPress is a powerful content management system (CMS) that allows for maximum customization. For a self-hosted option, consider WordPress.org.

Meet the Authors:

Meet the Authors is a service that provides tailored author websites. They focus on delivering a personalized experience that aligns with an author's unique style and brand.

rs

latform specifically designed for authors, websites with features like event sletters.

AuthorBrandCo specialises in author branding and website design. They work closely with authors to create visually stunning and effective websites.

Book Marketers:

Book Marketers is a company that offers a range of author services, including website design. They tailor their designs to meet the specific needs and branding of authors.

Before choosing a website design service, consider your specific needs, budget, and the level of customization you desire. Look for companies that understand the unique requirements of author websites and can effectively showcase your brand and books.

STEP 36 – CREATE YOUR MARKETING PLAN

Crafting a robust marketing plan is paramount for the successful launch and sustained visibility of a published book. In an increasingly competitive literary landscape, a well-thought-out marketing strategy acts as the guiding force behind reaching a wider audience. It serves to create anticipation and excitement around the book, ensuring that its unique value is communicated effectively. A comprehensive marketing plan not only introduces the work to potential readers but also builds a brand around the author, fostering a lasting connection with the audience. By strategically employing various promotional channels, from social media and author websites to book clubs and traditional media, a good marketing plan maximizes visibility, drives sales, and sets the stage for long-term success. It transforms the act of publishing a book from a solitary event into a dynamic, ongoing conversation between the author and their readership, ultimately contributing to the book's enduring impact.

1. Social Media Engagement:

Leverage the power of social media platforms like Instagram, Twitter, Facebook, and LinkedIn to connect with readers. Share visually appealing content, engage in conversations, and use targeted ads to reach specific demographics.

2. Author Website and Blog:

Establishing a professional author website serves as a central hub for readers. Regularly update a blog with engaging content, sneak peeks, and behind-the-scenes insights to keep the audience invested.

3. Email Marketing:

Build and maintain an email list to directly communicate with readers. Send newsletters containing exclusive content, promotions, and updates about upcoming releases.

4. Book Launch Events:

Organise virtual or in-person book launch events. These can include live readings, Q&A sessions, and giveaways to generate buzz and excitement around your book.

5. Book Reviews and Blog Tours:

Seek reviews from book bloggers, influential readers, and reputable literary critics. Arrange blog tours to amplify your book's visibility across various online platforms.

6. Book Clubs and Reading Groups:

Connect with book clubs and reading groups, either in person or online. Offer to join discussions, provide additional materials, or participate in Q&A sessions.

7. Utilise Book Platforms:

List your book on popular platforms like Goodreads Meet the Authors, BookBub, and LibraryThing. Engage with the communities on these platforms and take advantage of promotional opportunities.

8. Podcast Appearances:

Collaborate with podcasts related to your book's genre or themes. Share your writing journey, discuss your book, and tap into diverse audiences through this increasingly popular medium.

9. Online Bookstores and Retailers:

Optimise your book's presence on online bookstores like Amazon,

Barnes & Noble, and others. Utilise keywords, categories, and book descriptions to enhance discoverability.

10. Collaborate with Influencers:

Partner with influencers in your genre or industry for shoutouts, reviews, or collaborations. Their endorsement can significantly impact your book's visibility.

11. Paid Advertising:

Invest in targeted online advertising through platforms like Facebook Ads, Amazon Ads, and BookBub Featured Deals. Carefully craft ad copy and visuals to entice potential readers.

12. Local Community Engagement:

Connect with local bookstores, libraries, and community centres. Participate in book fairs, author signings, and events to build a local reader base.

13. Interactive Content:

Create interactive content such as quizzes, games, or exclusive digital experiences related to your book. This not only engages your audience but also encourages social sharing.

14. Collaborate with Other Authors:

Network with fellow authors for cross-promotions, joint events, or shared newsletters. Collaborative efforts can expand your reach to each other's audiences.

15. Continuous Adaptation:

Stay informed about emerging trends and technologies in book marketing. Be adaptable and open to trying new strategies as the landscape evolves.

In conclusion, successful book marketing involves a combination of traditional and digital methods, tailored to the author's strengths and the book's target audience. A diverse and integrated approach ensures a broader reach and increased opportunities for reader engagement.

STEP 37 – CONSIDER USING MARKETING ASSISTANCE

In the dynamic world of publishing, many authors turn to specialised companies to navigate the complexities of book marketing and promotion. These companies offer a range of services designed to enhance visibility, engage target audiences, and ultimately propel a book into the spotlight.

1. Publicity Firms:

Publicity firms specialise in securing media coverage for books. They cultivate relationships with journalists, arrange interviews, and coordinate features to generate buzz in traditional and online media.

2. Book Marketing Agencies:

Dedicated book marketing agencies provide end-to-end solutions, offering services like social media management, email marketing, advertising campaigns, and influencer outreach. They tailor strategies to align with an author's goals and target audience.

3. Virtual Book Tours:

Companies offering virtual book tours connect authors with bloggers, influencers, and online communities. These tours involve a series of online stops, including reviews, interviews, and guest posts, effectively expanding an author's digital footprint.

4. Book Publicists:

Book publicists focus on crafting compelling press releases, organizing book launch events, and securing media coverage. They play a crucial role in shaping an author's public image and getting their work noticed.

5. Online Review Services:

Platforms that provide paid review services connect authors with professional reviewers and readers. Positive reviews on reputable platforms can enhance a book's credibility and attract a broader readership.

6. BookBub and Similar Platforms:

Book promotion services like BookBub help authors reach a massive audience through targeted email newsletters and featured deals. These platforms have a significant impact on book sales and visibility.

7. Social Media Management Companies:

Social media management companies specialise in curating and executing effective social media strategies. They create engaging content, run targeted ads, and manage interactions, optimizing an author's online presence.

8. Book Launch Event Organizers:

Companies that specialise in organizing book launch events take care of the logistics involved in both virtual and in-person events. They ensure a seamless experience for authors and attendees, maximizing the event's impact.

9. Author Website Design Services:

Companies offering author website design services create visually appealing and functional websites tailored to an author's brand. An optimized website is crucial for effective online marketing.

10. Email Marketing Platforms:

Platforms like Mailchimp, ConvertKit, and others provide tools to streamline email marketing efforts. Authors can use these services to build and engage their reader mailing lists.

Leveraging these companies allows authors to tap into specialised expertise, saving time and effort while navigating the intricate landscape of book marketing. However, it's crucial for authors to thoroughly research and select services aligned with their goals, ensuring a tailored and effective promotional campaign for their unique literary work.

STEP 38 – RESEARCH INTO PLACING FACEBOOK ADVERTS

Crafting a Compelling Facebook Ad to Promote Your Book

Facebook Ads can be a powerful tool for reaching a vast audience and promoting your book effectively. Follow these steps to create an engaging and targeted Facebook Ad campaign:

Step 1: Define Your Objective
Before you start creating your ad, clarify your goal. Whether it's to drive book sales, increase website traffic, or boost your author page's followers, having a clear objective will guide the rest of your campaign.

Step 2: Identify Your Target Audience
Utilise Facebook's robust targeting options to reach the right audience. Define demographics, interests, and behaviours that align with your book's potential readers. Consider factors such as age, location, interests, and reading preferences.

Step 3: Create Eye-Catching Visuals
Design visually appealing ad creatives. Include high-quality images of your book cover, captivating visuals, and concise text. Ensure that the imagery reflects the tone and genre of your book. We will discuss this in detail in step 40.

Step 4: Craft Compelling Ad Copy
Write compelling ad copy that highlights the unique selling points of your book. Keep it concise, engaging, and focused on what makes your book a must-read. Use a clear call-to-action (CTA) to prompt users to take the desired action.

Step 5: Set a Budget and Schedule

Determine your advertising budget and the duration of your campaign. Facebook allows you to set a daily or lifetime budget. Experiment with different budget levels to find the balance between cost and reach that works for you.

Step 6: Choose Ad Placement
Decide where your ad will appear. Facebook offers various placement options, including the Facebook News Feed, Instagram, Audience Network, and more. Tailor your choices based on where your target audience is most likely to engage.

Step 7: Utilise Ad Formats
Experiment with different ad formats to see what resonates best with your audience. Carousel ads, slideshow ads, and video ads can provide dynamic ways to showcase your book and capture attention.

Step 8: Implement Tracking Pixels
Install Facebook Pixel on your website to track user interactions. This tool provides valuable data on ad performance, helping you refine your strategy based on user behaviour.

Step 9: Monitor and Optimise
Regularly monitor the performance of your Facebook Ad campaign. Analyse metrics such as click-through rates, engagement, and conversions. Use this data to make informed adjustments to your ad strategy.

Step 10: A/B Testing
Conduct A/B testing by creating variations of your ad to identify what resonates most with your audience. Test different visuals, ad copy, and CTAs to optimize your campaign over time.

Step 11: Engage with Comments
Respond to comments and engage with users who interact with your ad. Building a connection with your audience enhances the effectiveness of your campaign and fosters a sense of community.

By carefully planning and executing each step of your Facebook

Ad campaign, you can effectively promote your book to a targeted audience and generate meaningful engagement. Keep refining your approach based on the performance metrics and feedback to continually improve the impact of your Facebook Ads.

STEP 39 – RESEARCH INTO PLACING AMAZON ADVERTS

Amazon Ads are a powerful tool to increase the discoverability of your book on the world's largest online marketplace. Here's a step-by-step guide to creating an effective Amazon Ad campaign:

Step 1: Navigate to Amazon Advertising
Visit the Amazon Advertising platform (advertising.amazon.com) and sign in using your Amazon account. If you don't have an account, you'll need to create one.

Step 2: Choose Your Ad Type
Amazon offers different ad types, including Sponsored Products, Sponsored Brands, and Sponsored Display. For promoting a book, Sponsored Products and Sponsored Brands are commonly used. Sponsored Products showcase individual products, while Sponsored Brands allow you to promote a brand and feature multiple books.

Step 3: Select Your Campaign Type
Choose between "Automatic Targeting" and "Manual Targeting." Automatic Targeting lets Amazon determine where to display your ads based on relevant keywords, while Manual Targeting allows you to choose specific keywords yourself.

Step 4: Set Your Campaign Budget
Define your daily or lifetime budget for the campaign. Amazon Ads work on a pay-per-click (PPC) model, so you'll only pay when users click on your ad.

Step 5: Choose Your Targeting
If you opt for Manual Targeting, select relevant keywords related

to your book. For Automatic Targeting, Amazon will use its algorithms to target your ads based on your book's category, keywords, and product details.

Step 6: Set Your Bid
Determine the maximum amount you're willing to pay for a click. Your bid, combined with the relevance of your ad, influences its placement in search results and on product pages.

Step 7: Create Your Ad
Compose compelling ad copy and select high-quality images of your book cover. Ensure that your ad provides a clear and enticing message to potential readers. We will discuss this in detail in step 40.

Step 8: Monitor Your Ad Performance
Once your ad is live, regularly monitor its performance through the Amazon Advertising dashboard. Track metrics such as clicks, impressions, and conversion rates. We will go into this in detail in step 42.

Step 9: Adjust and Optimize
Based on the performance data, adjust your campaign. Refine your keywords, update ad copy, or adjust your bid to optimize your ad's effectiveness.

Step 10: Experiment with Ad Variations
Consider creating multiple ad variations to see which performs best. Experiment with different ad copy, images, and targeting strategies to identify the most successful approach for your book.

Step 11: Utilise Enhanced Brand Content (EBC) and A+ Content
If eligible, use Enhanced Brand Content (for registered brands) or A+ Content (for KDP authors) to enhance your book's detail page with additional images and text, providing a richer experience for potential readers.

By following these steps, you can create a targeted and compelling Amazon Ad campaign to boost the visibility of your book among potential readers on the Amazon platform. Regularly analyse performance metrics and refine your strategy to maximize the impact of your advertising efforts.

STEP 40 – DESIGNING ADVERTS

In the dynamic realm of book promotion and online presence, the significance of getting your advertising right cannot be overstated. Your advertising endeavours act as the linchpin in a digital landscape teeming with literary content, serving as the guiding force that directs potential readers to discover and engage with your book. Beyond mere visibility, a meticulously crafted advertising strategy is the linchpin that bridges the gap between your literary creation and its intended audience. It becomes the narrative thread that weaves your author brand into the vast tapestry of online content, creating an indelible mark on the minds of those you aim to captivate. Precision in advertising not only ensures that your promotional efforts are finely tuned to resonate with the right demographic but also establishes a nuanced connection with readers. This connection goes beyond the transactional, fostering a sense of community and loyalty that is pivotal for building a robust and enduring online presence. In essence, getting your advertising right is not just a promotional tactic; it's a strategic imperative that shapes the narrative of your author brand and lays the foundation for a lasting and meaningful relationship with your readership.

Dos for Effective Book Advertising and Online Presence:

1. **Define Clear Objectives**: Clearly outline your advertising goals. Whether it's driving book sales, increasing website traffic, or growing your social media following, having a well-defined objective guides your strategy.

2. **Know Your Audience:** Understand your target audience's

demographics, interests, and online behaviour. Tailor your advertising content to resonate with their preferences.

3. **Compelling Visuals and Copy**: Create visually striking and engaging ad creatives that align with your book's genre and message. Craft compelling ad copy that succinctly communicates the unique selling points of your book.

4. **Utilise Targeting Options**: Leverage the targeting capabilities of advertising platforms. Define specific demographics, interests, and keywords to ensure your ads reach the most relevant audience.

5. **Monitor and Analyse Metrics:** Regularly track key performance metrics such as click-through rates, impressions, and conversion rates. Use this data to assess the effectiveness of your campaigns and make informed adjustments.

6. **Experiment with A/B Testing:** Conduct A/B testing with variations in visuals, ad copy, and targeting parameters. This helps identify the most effective elements of your campaign for optimization.

7. **Optimise for Mobile**: Ensure your ads are optimized for mobile devices. With a significant portion of internet users accessing content on mobile, a mobile-friendly ad enhances user experience.

8. **Utilise Amazon Author Central and Enhanced Content**: If applicable, enhance your Amazon Author Central profile and Utilise features like Enhanced Brand Content (EBC) to provide additional information about yourself and your book.

Don'ts for Book Advertising and Online Presence:

1. **Overlook the Importance of Research:** Don't skip thorough research on your target audience and competitors. Understanding the market landscape is crucial for effective advertising.

2. Neglect Mobile Optimization: Don't disregard the significance of mobile optimization. Failing to cater to mobile users can result in a significant loss of potential engagement.

3. Ignore Analytics: Don't neglect monitoring and analysing your campaign's performance. Regularly assess data to identify trends, strengths, and areas for improvement.

4. Rely Solely on One Platform: Don't limit your advertising efforts to a single platform. Diversify your approach to reach a broader audience across various channels and platforms.

5. Misalign Ad Content with Book Genre: Avoid creating ads that misrepresent the genre or tone of your book. Ensuring alignment between the ad content and the book helps manage reader expectations.

6. Neglect Engagement: Don't view advertising as a one-way communication. Actively engage with your audience by responding to comments, questions, and reviews.

7. Overcomplicate Ad Copy: Keep ad copy concise and compelling. Avoid overloading it with information, as clarity and brevity enhance the impact of your message.

8. Underestimate the Power of Branding: Don't underestimate the importance of building and maintaining a strong author brand. Consistent branding across ads and online platforms fosters recognition and trust.

STEP 41 – ENHANCE YOUR AMAZON PRESENCE

In the ever-evolving landscape of modern literature, the importance of cultivating complete and appropriate author profiles on platforms such as Amazon and various social media cannot be overstated. Beyond the confines of the printed page, these digital realms have become pivotal spaces where authors forge connections with their readership. A robust author profile serves as a virtual calling card, offering a glimpse into the mind behind the words and providing readers with a richer, more immersive experience.

Creating a Digital Persona on Amazon:

Bridging the Gap Between Author and Reader:

An author's journey goes beyond the narratives they craft; it extends into the very fabric of their identity. On Amazon, a complete author profile serves as a bridge between the creative mind and the curious reader. When a potential reader stumbles upon a book, an enticing author profile beckons them to delve deeper into the creator's world. From the author's bio and photograph to links to personal websites and social media accounts, this comprehensive profile paints a vivid picture, offering insights into the author's inspirations, motivations, and the stories behind the stories.

Navigating the Literary Landscape:

For prolific authors with a repertoire of works, an Amazon author profile acts as a literary compass, guiding readers through the author's body of work. From bestselling novels to hidden gems, a well-curated profile serves as a curated exhibition of an author's literary journey. Readers can seamlessly navigate between works, discovering hidden gems or embarking on a journey from an author's debut to their latest masterpiece.

Building Trust and Credibility:

Trust is paramount in the world of literature. A complete and professionally presented author profile fosters credibility, signalling to readers that they are engaging with a legitimate and committed writer. Author profiles that include accolades, awards, and links to reputable sources further bolster the author's standing, cultivating a sense of trust and reliability in the eyes of the reader. **Crafting a Cohesive Social Media Presence:**

Tailoring Your Digital Persona:

Social media platforms offer authors an expansive canvas to paint a more dynamic and interactive portrait. Crafting a cohesive digital persona involves aligning the author's online presence with their unique voice and literary brand. From the choice of profile picture to the language used in bio sections, every element contributes to the author's distinct online identity.

Engaging with Readers:

Social media facilitates direct and immediate engagement with readers. Authors can share snippets of their writing process, offer behind-the-scenes glimpses, and participate in conversations with a global audience. A responsive and interactive author profile contributes to a vibrant literary community, allowing readers to feel connected to the person behind the words.

Amplifying Book Promotion:

Well-maintained social media profiles serve as dynamic platforms for book promotion. Authors can share updates about upcoming releases, post visually appealing content related to their books, and run targeted promotional campaigns. Leveraging the reach of social media platforms amplifies the visibility of an author's works, ensuring they resonate with a wider audience.

Showcasing Personality and Authenticity:

In a digital landscape saturated with content, authenticity stands out. A thoughtful author profile on social media should not merely be a promotional tool but a genuine expression of the author's personality. Sharing personal anecdotes, hobbies, and moments of vulnerability creates a more authentic connection with readers, fostering a community of loyal followers.

Navigating Challenges and Potential Pitfalls:

Balancing Personal and Professional:

Striking the right balance between personal and professional content is a nuanced challenge. While readers appreciate glimpses into an author's life, maintaining a level of professionalism is essential. Oversharing or veering too far into personal territory can dilute the author's brand and impact.

Managing Privacy and Boundaries:

Authors must navigate the delicate balance of sharing without compromising their privacy. Setting clear boundaries and being mindful of the information shared ensures a positive and secure online experience for both the author and their readers.

In the digital age, where readers crave not just stories but meaningful connections with the storytellers, author profiles on platforms like Amazon and social media serve as virtual portals. They invite readers to step into the author's world, fostering a sense of intimacy and shared literary exploration. Authors who invest time and thought into curating their digital personas reap the rewards of a vibrant and engaged readership, transcending the traditional author-reader relationship to build a global community united by a love for storytelling. Through these platforms, authors not only share their words but also become narrators of their own narratives, weaving a tapestry that extends far beyond the pages of their books. In essence, the importance of complete and appropriate author profiles lies in the profound impact they have on shaping the perception of the author, forging connections, and contributing to the rich tapestry of the literary landscape.

STEP 42 – MONITORING YOUR ADVERTS

Successfully placing, managing and optimising your advertising campaigns on platforms like Amazon and Facebook requires vigilant monitoring and strategic adjustments. Here's a comprehensive guide on how to effectively oversee your ad performance and implement rules to enhance your campaign's efficiency:

Amazon Ad Monitoring:

Regularly Check Campaign Metrics:

Keep a close eye on key metrics such as click-through rates (CTR), conversion rates, and ad spend. Amazon provides detailed analytics on your campaign's performance.

Monitor Search Term Reports:

Review search term reports to identify which keywords are driving clicks and conversions. Adjust your keyword strategy based on this data to refine targeting.

Analyse Product Detail Page Views:

Track the number of product detail page views generated by your ads. An increase in page views may indicate user interest, while a low number may require adjustments.

Watch Competitor Activity:

Keep an eye on your competitors' products and ad strategies. Understand how their presence may impact your campaign and adapt your approach accordingly.

Adjust Bids Based on Performance:

Regularly adjust your keyword bids based on performance data. Increase bids for high-performing keywords and consider lowering bids for those with lower returns.

Optimize Ad Copy and Imagery:

Continuously test and optimize your ad copy and imagery. A/B testing different creatives can help identify which elements resonate best with your audience.

Utilise Negative Keywords:

Implement negative keywords to exclude irrelevant search terms. This helps improve the relevance of your ads and reduces wasted ad spend.

Monitor Product Availability:

Ensure that advertised products are consistently in stock. Pausing ads for out-of-stock items prevents disappointed customers and maximizes your ad budget.

Amazon Ad Rules:

Rule: Adjust Bids Based on ACoS:

Condition: If your Advertising Cost of Sales (ACoS) exceeds a predefined threshold.

Action: Automatically adjust bids for keywords contributing to a high ACoS to improve profitability.

Rule: Pause Low-Performing Keywords:

Condition: If a keyword has a low CTR or has not generated conversions.

Action: Automatically pause or lower bids for underperforming keywords to allocate budget to more effective ones.

Rule: Daily Budget Adjustments:

Condition: If daily spend consistently exceeds or falls below a set budget.

Action: Automatically adjust daily budgets to ensure optimal spending while avoiding overspending or underspending.

Facebook Ad Monitoring:

Review Facebook Ad Insights:

Regularly check Facebook Ad Insights for metrics like reach, engagement, and conversion rates. Identify trends and areas for improvement.

Analyse Audience Insights:

Utilise Facebook Audience Insights to understand your audience's demographics, interests, and behaviour. Refine your targeting based on this information.

Monitor Ad Placement Performance:

Evaluate the performance of your ads on different placements (e.g., News Feed, Instagram, Audience Network). Adjust bids and budgets based on placement effectiveness.

Test Different Ad Formats:

Experiment with various ad formats, including images, videos, and carousels. Analyse which formats resonate best with your audience and allocate budget accordingly.

Watch Frequency and Ad Fatigue:

Keep an eye on ad frequency to avoid ad fatigue. High frequency can lead to decreased effectiveness. Implement rules to refresh ad creatives or adjust targeting.

Utilise A/B Testing:

Set up A/B tests for ad creatives, copy, and audiences. Evaluate performance variations and use the results to refine and optimize your campaigns.

Optimize Landing Pages:

Ensure your landing pages are optimised for conversions. A well-designed and responsive landing page contributes to a seamless user experience.

Facebook Ad Rules:

Rule: Pause Underperforming Ad Sets:

Condition: If an ad set consistently fails to meet predefined performance metrics.

Action: Automatically pause or adjust budget for underperforming ad sets to reallocate resources.

Rule: Bid Adjustments Based on ROAS:

Condition: If Return on Ad Spend (ROAS) falls below or exceeds a specified threshold.

Action: Automatically adjust bids to optimize for the desired ROAS and improve campaign profitability.

Rule: Dynamic Creative Optimization:

Condition: If certain ad creatives consistently outperform others.

Action: Utilise dynamic creative optimization rules to automatically prioritize and allocate budget to high-performing creatives.

Rule: Schedule Ad Placements:

Condition: Based on historical data, identify peak times for engagement.

Action: Schedule ad placements during high-engagement periods to maximize visibility and interactions.

By diligently monitoring and implementing rules for your Amazon and Facebook ad campaigns, you can maintain a proactive approach to optimization. Regular adjustments based on performance data ensure that your advertising strategy remains agile and aligned with your goals, ultimately maximizing the impact of your campaigns.

STEP 43 – WAITING FOR REVIEWS

Embarking on the journey of releasing your first book is an exhilarating experience, and as anticipation builds, so does the eagerness to receive feedback, especially in the form of reviews. Waiting for those initial reviews can be both exciting and nerve-wracking, as authors eagerly seek validation for their creative endeavours. However, it's crucial to approach this period with patience, resilience, and an understanding that the reception of your work is subjective.

Embrace the Process:

The period after releasing your book is a time of suspense, and waiting for the first reviews is part of the natural rhythm of becoming a published author. Embrace this waiting phase as an opportunity for personal growth and reflection on your journey as a writer.

Patience is a Virtue:

Rome wasn't built in a day, and neither are literary legacies. Understand that garnering reviews takes time. Readers, much like authors, have their own schedules, and it may take a while for your book to find its way onto their reading list. Be patient and let the organic process unfold.

Diverse Perspectives Await:

Anticipate a range of responses to your work. Every reader brings their unique set of preferences, experiences, and perspectives to the table. Some may resonate deeply with your narrative, while others may not connect as profoundly. Embrace the diversity of opinions that will inevitably surface.

The Power of Constructive Criticism:

Negative feedback, though initially disheartening, can be a valuable source of growth. Look beyond the emotional sting and seek constructive elements within critical reviews. Constructive criticism often holds nuggets of insight that can guide your evolution as a writer.

A Lesson in Subjectivity:

Remember that literary taste is inherently subjective. What doesn't resonate with one reader may profoundly touch another. The beauty of diversity in reading preferences highlights the richness and complexity of the literary world. Appreciate the varied ways in which readers interpret and engage with your work.

Maintaining Resilience:

Negativity, whether constructive or not, can be challenging to digest. However, resilience is the author's greatest ally. Understand that not every reader will be your ideal audience, and that's perfectly okay. Use criticism as fuel to refine your craft and continue evolving as a writer.

Celebrating Positive Feedback:

Celebrate and savour the positive reviews that undoubtedly will come your way. Revel in the joy of connecting with readers who resonate with your storytelling. Positive feedback can be a powerful motivator, affirming that your work has made a meaningful impact.

The Long-Term Perspective:

Reviews, especially in the digital age, are continuous and ever evolving. What may be a lukewarm review today can transform into a glowing recommendation tomorrow. Keep a long-term perspective, understanding that your book will continue to find its audience over time.

Connecting with Your Readership:

Engage with your readers, both those who praise and those who critique. Building a genuine connection with your audience fosters a sense of community and loyalty. Responding to reviews, expressing gratitude, and being open to dialogue humanizes the author-reader relationship.

In the intricate dance between author and reader, waiting for those first reviews is a significant step. Approach this juncture with a spirit of resilience, understanding that every review, positive or negative, is a contribution to your journey as a writer. The diverse tapestry of reader responses is a testament to the multifaceted nature of literature and the dynamic relationship between authors and their audience.

STEP 44 – TRYING TO GET YOUR BOOK INTO BOOKSTORES AND LIBRARIES

Securing placement in libraries and bookstores is a pivotal step for any author aspiring to reach a wider audience. Here's a strategic guide on how to increase the chances of getting your book onto the shelves of these literary havens:

1. Research Your Target Libraries and Bookstores:

Libraries: Identify libraries that align with your book's genre, theme, or subject matter. Research their acquisition policies, reading programs, and contact information for submission.

Bookstores: Explore independent bookstores, chain book retailers, and specialty stores that cater to your book's niche. Understand their submission guidelines and preferred genres.

2. Prepare a Professional Book Proposal:

Libraries: Craft a comprehensive book proposal that includes a concise summary, information about your target audience, and reasons why your book would be a valuable addition to their collection.

Bookstores: Prepare a press kit that includes an eye-catching book cover, a compelling author bio, and positive reviews or endorsements if available. This kit serves as a snapshot of your book's marketability.

3. Leverage Author Platforms:

Libraries: Establish a presence on library-focused platforms such as NetGalley, where librarians can discover and review your book. Participate in library events and engage with librarian communities online.

Bookstores: Utilise your author's website, social media, and book launch events to showcase your book. A strong online presence can attract the attention of bookstore buyers.

4. Connect with Librarians and Booksellers:

Libraries: Attend library conferences, networking events, and engage with librarians on social media. Personal connections can significantly impact the likelihood of your book being considered.

Bookstores: Establish relationships with local booksellers by attending book fairs, signings, and participating in community events. A personal connection can make a difference in stocking decisions.

5. Utilise Distribution Services:

Libraries: Consider utilizing library distribution services that facilitate the inclusion of your book in library catalogues. Services like Baker & Taylor or OverDrive connect authors with library systems.

Bookstores: Work with book distributors and wholesalers who can help get your book into the hands of retailers. Companies like IngramSpark or BookBaby offer distribution services.

6. Participate in Local Author Programs:

Libraries: Many libraries have programs that feature local authors. Inquire about participating in book readings, discussions, or workshops to gain visibility.

Bookstores: Contact local bookstores and inquire about their support for local authors. Offer to organize book signings or other events that can draw attention to your book.

7. Leverage Book Awards and Reviews:

Libraries: Submit your book for consideration in library-focused book awards. Winning or being shortlisted can significantly increase the visibility of your book.

Bookstores: Positive reviews and accolades lend credibility to your book. Seek reviews from reputable sources and prominently display endorsements on your book cover and marketing materials.

8. Offer Special Promotions:

Libraries: Create promotional packages or discounts specifically for libraries. Highlight any study guide or book club resources that accompany your book.

Bookstores: Run limited-time promotions, discounts, or exclusive content offers to incentivize bookstores to stock your book.

9. Utilise Self-Publishing Platforms:

Libraries: Ensure your book is available through self-publishing platforms that libraries commonly use. Platforms like OverDrive or Biblioboard specialize in library distribution.

Bookstores: Make your book available through popular self-publishing platforms that bookstores trust, such as IngramSpark.

10. Persistence Pays Off:

Libraries and Bookstores: Rejections are part of the journey. If your book doesn't get accepted initially, don't be disheartened. Keep refining your approach, seeking feedback, and persistently pursuing opportunities.

By strategically navigating the submission process and proactively engaging with the literary community, you can enhance the visibility of your book and increase the likelihood of it finding a place on the shelves of both libraries and bookstores. Remember, persistence and a well-prepared approach can make a significant difference in gaining entry to these literary gateways.

STEP 45 – CONSIDER AN IN PERSON OR VIRTUAL BOOK SIGNING

Arranging a book signing or a virtual book signing event is an exciting opportunity to connect directly with readers and showcase your work. Here's a strategic guide on how to secure these events, whether in-person or in the digital realm:

1. Research and Identify Suitable Venues:

In-Person Book Signings: Identify local bookstores, libraries, or literary events that align with your book's genre or theme. Reach out to these venues with a proposal for a book signing event.

Virtual Book Signings: Explore online platforms that host virtual book events. Consider partnering with virtual book clubs, literary festivals, or book-focused websites.

2. Craft a Compelling Proposal:

In-Person Book Signings: Create a professional proposal that includes details about your book, a brief author bio, and reasons why your book signing would benefit the venue and its audience.

Virtual Book Signings: Develop a proposal tailored for virtual events, highlighting the interactive elements you can bring to the online space. Emphasize how your virtual presence can engage a wide audience.

3. Utilize Author Platforms:

In-Person Book Signings: Leverage your author platform to demonstrate your following and engagement. Highlight your social media presence, email subscribers, and any previous successful events.

Virtual Book Signings: Promote your virtual event through your website, social media, and mailing list. A strong online presence can attract participants to your virtual book signing.

4. Engage with Local Communities:

In-Person Book Signings: Engage with local book clubs, writing groups, or community organizations. Building connections within your community can lead to opportunities for book signings.

Virtual Book Signings: Collaborate with online communities, book clubs, or forums related to your book's genre. Engaging with these communities can help generate interest in your virtual event.

5. Partner with Bookstores and Libraries:

In-Person Book Signings: Forge partnerships with local bookstores or libraries to host your event. Bookstore managers and librarians may appreciate the opportunity to feature local authors.

Virtual Book Signings: Partner with online bookstores or libraries to host virtual book signing events. Collaborative efforts can broaden your reach and attract a diverse audience.

6. Offer Exclusive Content:

In-Person Book Signings: Consider offering exclusive content or incentives for attendees, such as signed bookplates, bookmarks, or limited-edition materials.

Virtual Book Signings: Provide digital perks, like downloadable extras, exclusive Q&A sessions, or personalized virtual interactions for attendees who participate in your virtual book signing.

7. Create an Event Proposal:

In-Person Book Signings: Draft an event proposal outlining the logistics, including the date, time, expected attendance, and any special requests. Address how your event will benefit the venue.

Virtual Book Signings: Develop a virtual event proposal that outlines the format, technology requirements, and potential engagement activities. Clearly convey the value of your virtual presence.

8. Leverage Book Clubs:

In-Person Book Signings: Connect with local book clubs and propose your book as a featured selection. Many book clubs appreciate the opportunity to meet the author in person.

Virtual Book Signings: Offer your book to virtual book clubs and suggest a virtual author discussion or Q&A session. Virtual book clubs can provide a platform for engaging discussions.

9. Engage Your Network:

In-Person Book Signings: Encourage friends, family, and followers to spread the word about your book signing. Word of mouth can be a powerful tool in attracting attendees.

Virtual Book Signings: Leverage your online network to promote the virtual event. Encourage followers to share the event details on social media and participate in the virtual book signing.

10. Be Flexible and Adaptable:

In-Person Book Signings: Be flexible with event dates and times to accommodate the venue's schedule. Adapt to any requirements or preferences the venue may have.

Virtual Book Signings: Embrace different virtual platforms and be adaptable to various formats. Consider the preferences of your audience and the hosting platform.

Securing book signings, whether in-person or virtual, requires a combination of preparation, networking, and effective communication. By strategically approaching potential venues and showcasing the unique value of your book and presence, you can increase your chances of hosting successful events that leave a lasting impact on readers.

STEP 46 – HAVE YOU TOLD THE ENTIRE STORY?

Heartfelt congratulations on reaching this incredible milestone—the completion of your journey from the inception of an idea to the triumphant release of your first book. Your dedication to not only writing but also navigating the intricate processes of editing, publishing, and marketing is a testament to your passion and resilience as an author. Welcome to the club.

As you reflect on this momentous achievement, I invite you to pause and bask in the well-deserved glow of accomplishment. You've breathed life into characters, woven intricate plots, and introduced readers to worlds of your creation. It's a remarkable feat, one that deserves celebration and acknowledgment.

Now, as you stand on the summit of this literary conquest, take a moment to ponder: Is your story truly complete? Have all the narratives been told, or do some characters linger, whispering of untold adventures and unexplored territories? Is there a sequel waiting to burst forth from the confines of your imagination?

Consider the questions left unanswered, the characters poised and ready for new exploits. Your first book is a testament to your storytelling prowess, and it may have laid the foundation for a universe brimming with possibilities. Are there loose ends that crave resolution? Are there new worlds waiting to be discovered? Does a fresh narrative itch to be written, eager to captivate the hearts and minds of your readers once more?

As you revel in the success of your debut, entertain the notion of embarking on a new literary journey. The prospect of writing a second book may seem daunting, yet it holds the promise of further artistic evolution and storytelling brilliance. You've honed your craft, faced the challenges of publication, and navigated the intricacies of marketing. Now, armed with experience and a proven voice, imagine the wonders your next tale could unveil.

Is it time to do it all again? To craft new characters, delve into uncharted narratives, and weave another tapestry of emotions and adventures? Your first book was a chapter in your authorial odyssey—now, the blank pages of a second book beckon, inviting you to explore, create, and share once more.

Embrace the excitement of a new beginning and may your second book be as captivating and fulfilling as the first. The literary world eagerly awaits the next chapter of your storytelling journey.

Congratulations once again, and here's to the endless possibilities that lie ahead!

ABOUT THE AUTHORS

Created by co-founders Lee Davies and Robert Jones, two everyday authors from the UK. Lee Davies is the author of The Utopia Conspiracy and Robert Jones is the author of the Micklegate series. Together, they use their years of experience to create how-to guides, with step-by-step training and tools to help authors on their literary journey. Whether you need help with writing, editing, publishing, marketing or anything else related to being an author, you can find it on ASPA. You can also join the Forum, a community where you can request advice and also help others with your own insights and tips.

Printed in Great Britain
by Amazon